Endeavor®

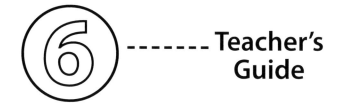

6 ------- Teacher's
Guide

New Readers Press®
ProLiteracy's publishing division

Endeavor® 6: Teacher's Guide
ISBN 978-1-56420-874-3

Copyright © 2009 New Readers Press
New Readers Press
ProLiteracy's Publishing Division
104 Marcellus Street, Syracuse, New York 13204
www.newreaderspress.com

Printed in the United States of America
16

Proceeds from the sale of New Readers Press materials support professional development, training, and technical assistance programs of ProLiteracy that benefit local literacy programs in the U.S. and around the globe.

Contributing Author: Vista Resources, Inc.
Developmental Editors: Ellen Northcott, Donna Townsend
Creative Director: Andrea Woodbury
Production Specialist: Maryellen Casey

Contents

Strategies for Success with *Endeavor*

Tips for Planning Instruction

There are a number of strategies that you can implement to maximize the effectiveness of *Endeavor's* lesson plans. First, always prepare your lessons before class. This includes reading and practicing the text of the story, selecting activities, and preparing materials. Although the *Endeavor* Teacher's Guide is intended to provide ideas and guidance, it is not meant as a script. Use the explanations in the Teacher's Guide to help you develop explanations in your own words. Additionally, modify the questions, examples, and activities to suit the needs of your students. If, for example, some students need more time to complete an element in the lesson, determine which activities you can omit or shortcut in order for students to have the time they need to be successful. Remember, the objective is for students to feel satisfaction as they become aware of their gains in building reading, writing, and other language skills.

Tips for Implementing Instruction

Students should be clear about what is expected of them. Therefore, inform students of the learning goals and outcomes before beginning a lesson. This Teacher's Guide provides learning objectives on the first page of notes for each lesson. Students should also be clear about how they will perform the tasks required of them. It is imperative, therefore, that you model every new skill, and model skills again if your students have not practiced them in a while. For example, model a sentence that uses a new vocabulary word correctly and in a meaningful context, and then work with students to explain what made your sentence effective. This kind of explicit skill modeling will make your expectations clear to your students. Students will begin to internalize what constitutes a complete answer or a meaningful interaction with a text.

In addition to modeling skills, you will also want to model strategies. Create your own Think About Its to complement those incorporated in the student book. Modeling how you think as you read will provide students with concrete examples of the ways that they should be interacting with text. If you realize that your students have never taken notes as they read, model notetaking. Use a text photocopied onto an overhead transparency and demonstrate how you highlight relevant passages or take notes on the side of the text. The more specific you are and the more examples you give of the various skills and strategies, the clearer the understanding will be in students' minds. Use of the active reading strategies should become second nature to students. This will occur with repetition, so remind them to use strategies that they have already learned.

Fluency and vocabulary development are important components of your students' reading growth. Therefore, you and your students should read aloud whenever possible. Not only will students get to listen to your fluent model and practice their own oral fluency, but students' reading will provide an opportunity for you to do informal assessments. Similarly, the Vocabulary Knowledge Rating Chart (Master 9) can help you to assess your students' facility with words and can inform your vocabulary instruction. If, for instance, most of your students indicate that they fully understand the word *bruised*, but the word *permeated* is unfamiliar, spend your instructional time on the unfamiliar word. Additionally, spend more time on the words that students are likely to encounter in a variety of texts—the key vocabulary words—rather than specialized vocabulary. There are activities and suggestions throughout the Teacher's Guide to assist you in your explanations and planning.

Tips for Maximizing Students as Resources

The life experience of adult learners is invaluable, so make sure that you are bringing students' prior knowledge into every aspect of your teaching. Make your examples relevant to students' experience, and allow them to draw connections between what they are learning and what they already know. The stories and articles in *Endeavor* were selected because they are likely in some way to relate to students' life experiences and concerns. Find those connections, and make them clear to students.

In addition to utilizing students' prior knowledge in your lessons, use students as resources for themselves and one another. The Revising and Editing Checklist (Master 11) is provided as a tool for students. They can check and improve their own and their peers' work using very specific criteria. As always, model the use of the Revising and Editing Checklist, and give students ample opportunity to practice with it. Also, have students use the Writing Rubric (Master 10) to evaluate their completed pieces against measures of ideas, organization, voice, and conventions. Compare your evaluations with theirs as part of writing conferences. These strategies for self- and peer-evaluation do not preclude the need for teacher assessment, but they do give students another set of eyes as they review their own work. The Revising and Editing Checklist and the Writing Rubric allow students to work with and eventually internalize criteria for an acceptable piece of writing.

Assessment is the key to determining if your instruction has been successful and if your students are progressing. You should be using periodic formal assessments, such as the TABE (Tests of Adult Basic Education) or another instrument, to track your students' progress. Informal assessments are important as well, particularly when it comes to modifying your instruction from lesson to lesson. Informal assessments include checklists of skills, over-the-shoulder analyses of students' reading, and your evaluations of students' class work. Although *Endeavor* provides rich resources in terms of texts, activities, strategies, and pedagogy, ultimately it is you, the teacher, who is most important to your students' success. It is your preparation, modeling, and evaluation that will ensure that your students are growing as learners, readers, and writers. We welcome you and wish you luck as you embark on this *Endeavor*.

Suggestions for Developing Vocabulary

Key Vocabulary

The key vocabulary words have been chosen because they are likely to be entirely unfamiliar or somewhat unfamiliar to many students. By working with these words before students begin reading, you are giving students additional keys with which to unlock the meaning of the text. The more they know before reading, the more they are likely to take with them from the reading.

In addition to helping students comprehend a particular text, vocabulary study will provide students with new words to add to their working vocabularies. As their vocabularies grow, they will be able to read increasingly more complex texts. They will also be able to express themselves in a more sophisticated manner in their writing and speaking.

Side-Column Vocabulary

Vocabulary words can be broken down into three tiers. Tier 1 words are the most basic words. These words (like *crumpled, nodded,* and *future*) do not need to be taught, because they are already part of students' vocabularies. Tier 2 words (like *meticulously, permeated,* and *preceding*) are found in more sophisticated texts and across a variety of domains. These are the kinds of words that have been selected as key vocabulary words.

Tier 3 words (like *bodega, merchandise,* and *retailers*) are specialized vocabulary. These words appear infrequently in texts and generally apply only to specific domains. These are the kinds of words that have been selected as side-column vocabulary. Although it will be useful to teach these words in the context of the particular text you are reading, they are not likely to appear frequently or in a variety of texts. Therefore, *Endeavor* focuses more on direct instruction and practice of Tier 2 words than it does on Tier 3 words.

How to Use the Vocabulary Knowledge Rating Chart

The Vocabulary Knowledge Rating Chart (Master 9) is a quick tool for determining students' prior knowledge of each of the vocabulary words. Not only will it help students focus on each of the words, but it will give you a sense of the words on which you will want to concentrate instruction.

Model the use of the Vocabulary Knowledge Rating Chart when you first introduce it. Once students are familiar with the chart, however, they should be able to use it on subsequent sets of words quickly and without extensive instruction.

Tips for Teaching Vocabulary

- The key to learning vocabulary is practice. Each lesson guide includes a number of different strategies for vocabulary practice. Provide as many opportunities as possible for students to interact with and practice the new words.

- Be sure to reframe students' sentences if they are using words incorrectly, and provide additional examples and explanations if necessary. If students learn vocabulary words incorrectly, they will use them incorrectly in the future.

- Use challenging vocabulary when you are talking to your students. Your modeling will help them use words in appropriate contexts, and the unfamiliar words you use will encourage students to explore vocabulary beyond what is being explicitly taught.

- Encourage students to use their new vocabulary words in their everyday lives, and invite them to share anecdotes of when they use the words or encounter the words in conversations or in the media.

Suggestions for Keeping Personal Dictionaries

Personal dictionaries are meant both as spelling aids and as places to record and explore new vocabulary words. For maximum benefit, personal dictionaries should be user-friendly.

A personal dictionary can be created from a notebook or from paper stapled or bound together. It should be its own entity rather than part of another notebook. This will make it more easily accessible and portable as students move through various levels of *Endeavor*. The personal dictionary should be organized alphabetically and have at least four full pages for each letter, perhaps fewer for the less frequently used letters.

Since vocabulary words are best internalized when they are used often, it is important that personal dictionaries be interactive. Students should enter new words they encounter from their experience and from the texts and other print material they are reading. Ask them to include a clear definition and part of speech along with sentences, examples, sketches, or other means for them to internalize

a full, clear meaning of the term. Students should have a voice in deciding what to include in an entry.

Plan frequent activities that require students to return to the words they have recorded. Have students find a "k" word and share it with a neighbor; dramatize a "p" word and have the class guess it; sketch a simple drawing of a word; or write a sentence, correctly using at least three of their vocabulary words. If students simply enter the words and never return to them, the benefit of the personal dictionary will be minimal.

Inside the front and back covers of the personal dictionary, have students record words that are particularly challenging for them to spell. This will limit the number of times they need to search for those words in a large dictionary. It also gives the teacher a place to record words that students are consistently misspelling in their writing. Finally, it ensures that the personal dictionary is being utilized often, as it will be on students' desks as they are writing.

Suggestions for Writing Portfolios

A writing portfolio is intended to hold student work so that the student, teacher, or observer can see how the student has developed as a writer. A portfolio can be a file folder, a box, or a large envelope. Ask each student to create his or her own portfolio. Portfolios can include any writing that the student has done. If the class is producing

a lot of work, you will want to pick and choose items for the portfolio so that it doesn't become unmanageable and unusable. Encourage students to include pieces that they are particularly proud of. The goal is to have the contents organized and accessible.

By reviewing their portfolios, students, and particularly adult students, will have the opportunity to evaluate their own work and growth. They will also have access to the teacher's observations and evaluations of their work. Moreover, portfolios might include copies of the Writing Rubric (Master 10) which students can use to evaluate and comment on their own work. Self-evaluations of final drafts of writing can be modeled by the teacher and done often.

Writing portfolios should be interactive rather than stored out of reach. Students use them to review their work and note their progress. In addition, students should have the opportunity to return to a piece they have written, work to improve it, and then publish it in a creative way. By continuing to interact with their writing and evaluating their own progress, students will remain motivated to improve their writing.

Developing Fluency

Fluency is a reader's ability to recognize words automatically and accurately and to read aloud with appropriate expression. The expression is called *prosody*, and it includes intonation, stress, rate, rhythm, and phrasing. Prosody is important to a reader's understanding of the text. Students must comprehend what they are reading in addition to reading quickly and accurately; therefore, teachers must effectively model and teach prosody. And students need repetition in order to develop fluency.

Although the teacher is an important model of fluent reading, the teacher cannot work individually with every student at the same time. Also, in any group of readers, there are likely to be some differences in students' ability to read orally. Therefore, strategies have been developed to help classrooms of readers at different levels to work on fluency simultaneously. These strategies usually include modeling and repetition.

Fluency in *Endeavor*

Endeavor supports you as you work with your students to improve their fluency. Each lesson in the Teacher's Guide provides strategies you can use to practice fluency. With any of the texts, you may wish to use other strategies in addition to those described in the lesson.

Strategies

Echo Reading—With Echo Reading, students imitate fluent reading modeled by the teacher. The teacher reads aloud, and the students are the echo. Depending upon the level of the readers in your class, you will break the

text into phrases or full sentences. Read the phrase or sentence aloud, paying careful attention to your accuracy and prosody. Then have the class repeat the phrase or sentence, also paying careful attention to accuracy and prosody. Continue reading aloud and having the class echo you for the rest of the passage. Be sure to break the text at logical points in order to maintain the meaning of the text.

Choral Reading—Choral Reading involves students reading aloud together, like a chorus. The teacher begins by reading the chosen passage aloud, concentrating on accuracy and prosody. Then students read the same passage aloud in groups ranging from three students to the whole class reading together. In order to set and maintain the pace, the teacher reads aloud with the students. Choral Reading allows readers the opportunity to practice fluency in a situation where they are supported by other readers.

Paired Repeated Reading—Paired Repeated Reading involves students working with one another—rather than one-on-one with the teacher—in order to improve their fluency. Students work in pairs, and each partner selects a passage to read aloud. Students begin by reading their passages silently. Then partners take turns being the reader or listener. Readers read their passages aloud three times. After the first reading, the listener does not provide feedback. After the second and third readings, the listener provides feedback to the reader.

Be sure to explain and model for students how to give one another constructive feedback. Model directly for students, using a volunteer reader. Tell students that comments such as, "I didn't know from your reading that this sentence was a question" or "I could understand you better if you slowed down and read louder" are more helpful than "Good job." Do a *fishbowl* exercise where the class observes a pair of readers and the class gives feedback on the pairs' feedback to one another. Once students are clear on how to give each other feedback, you will not have to repeat the modeling or fishbowl.

Reading to the Teacher—With small numbers of students in a class, it is possible to give regular attention on fluency to individual students. This gives you a clear sense of each student's strengths and weaknesses. Have students choose passages. Give them an opportunity to review them before they read them aloud to you. Give specific and constructive feedback on accuracy and prosody immediately after the reading. You can also use Echo Reading one-on-one to give students the opportunity for repetition.

Popcorn Reading—With popcorn reading, students take turns reading aloud. Students do not know who is going to be reading next, just as you do not know which kernel of corn will pop next. One student reads a sentence, a few sentences, or a paragraph. Then, he or she says "Popcorn, . . ." and calls another student's name. That student reads part of the passage and then *popcorns* someone else. Students stay on their toes, because they do not know who will be reading next.

Performance Reading—Many students enjoy working in pairs or small groups to dramatize the text they are reading. This strategy works well with texts that include a lot of dialogue. Assign students different roles, and have them practice the dialogue for their characters so that they are able to read their parts fluently and with expression from the text. Then have students perform for the class.

Fluency Tips for the Teacher

- Read and prepare the text before coming to class. It is easier to model fluency if you are already familiar with the text.

- Make sure students are familiar with the text before they begin to work on fluency. If students have already worked with the vocabulary and content of the text, they will struggle less with pronunciation and phrasing.

- You can use different fluency strategies with the same text. On one day, you might choose to use Echo Reading with a particular story; the next day, you might choose a passage from the same story and do Choral Reading. Remember that repetition is one of the keys to enhancing fluency.

- When pairing students, split the class into two groups according to reading ability. Have the top student of your more able readers work with the top student of your less able readers (conversely, have the low student of your best readers work with the lowest student of your lowest readers.) This may minimize frustration while still providing readers with support.

Keeping Track of Students' Progress

You will want to keep track of your students' reading progress. You can do this by informally recording each individual student's reading accuracy.

- Begin by choosing an unfamiliar passage of about 200 words in length that is at the student's reading level (perhaps from the next lesson in his or her student book or from the student books above or below that level.) Have the student read the passage aloud to you.

- On a separate copy of the same text, put a check mark over each word that is properly read. Each time a reader substitutes, omits, or inserts a word, count it as an error. If the student corrects herself, do not count those words as errors.

- Tally the errors and determine the percentage of words that were accurately read.

- Record a student's reading accuracy every few weeks in order to track progress.

Note: Running Records can be used to do a more thorough analysis of a student's reading and enable you to address individual challenges. You can go online to find explanations and examples of Running Records.

Smart Eating

Lesson Overview: (PAGE 5)

Theme

Have students read the lesson title on page 5 and tell them that the title introduces the lesson theme, Health. Discuss the theme by having students make personal connections, telling what they do to stay healthy, and talking about people they know who are overweight and the health issues those people face.

Learning objectives

Be sure students understand the outcome of each of the learning goals.

- *Learn about childhood obesity.* Tell students that this article is about what people can do to keep their children healthy. Point out that the vocabulary and writing assignments relate to the theme of health and weight.
- *Learn to identify main idea and details.*
- *Master the key vocabulary used in the article.*
- *Write an explanation of how a parent can help an obese child lose weight.*

Preteach the vocabulary. (PAGE 5)

Read the key vocabulary words and their definitions to the students. Tell them that they will recognize all these words in the article.

- Distribute the Vocabulary Knowledge Rating Chart (Master 9) and have students individually rate each of the key vocabulary words.
- Review particularly challenging words with students by listing each one on the board, modeling its use in a sentence, and having two or three students use the word in original sentences. Reframe student sentences that do not use the new words correctly.

You may wish to offer a mini-lesson on nouns as students read the respective parts of speech with the definitions of the vocabulary words. [See page 39 of this book for a mini-lesson on nouns. Use Master 1 or 2 to give students practice in recognizing nouns.]

Before You Read (PAGE 6)

Explain that good readers get involved with what they read. Suggest that they develop the habit of reading with a pencil and sticky notes or a small notebook available. They will find that it is always helpful to highlight, underline, and write responses or questions as they read. An involved reader goes back to review his or her notes and markings after reading the passage. In this case, the highlighted information will also help students with their writing activities.

As students begin to write answers to the questions for each element on page 6, have them read the respective Think About Its.

Make predictions while you read. Have students read the first paragraph of "Goodbye Cookies, Hello Apples," and then read the Think About It. Point out that most nonfiction articles give information to the reader. Ask students to predict what information this article is likely to include. Will information about helping a child develop healthier eating habits be useful or relevant to them? Remind students that, as they read, they should check to see if their predictions were correct.

Use what you know. Use the Think About It to elicit discussion about children or adults they know who are overweight or who have other health problems. Encourage students to comment on how people they know have worked to improve their own health. The connections they make will help them to understand the text more fully.

Reading the Article (PAGES 7–9)

The article "Goodbye Cookies, Hello Apples" includes information about the risks of obesity and how a parent can help an obese child to reduce his or her weight.

Model for students how to pick out important information that answers these two questions: *What health risks do obese children face as they become adults?* and *How can a parent help an obese child to lose weight?* By having students use two different-colored highlighters—one to highlight answers to each question—students will be able to recall the details that support each main idea. Model for students an example of highlighting a phrase, such as "made wiser food choices and became more active" on page 7. Explain that it is important not to highlight too much; otherwise, highlighting becomes confusing.

Side-Column Vocabulary Remind students that the vocabulary words and phrases in the side column have been selected as important to the theme and content of the article. These words may be useful in the context of health, but they are not necessarily part of everyday language.

Mid-Passage Questions The answers to some of the questions are largely students' opinions, so there are not many right or wrong answers. Review students' written answers to assess whether they are getting meaning from the text. They should indicate in their answers that Shakira's mother is worried because Shakira is overweight. She decides to make changes in the family's nutrition and activity levels. As a result, Shakira loses weight, becomes healthier, and feels better about herself.

After You Read (PAGES 10–11)

Build a robust vocabulary. Direct students to check their answers in the answer keys in their books.

Think about your reading. Ask students to check their answers in the answer keys in their books. Ask additional questions to enrich the discussion so that students will be better able to write about fighting obesity. Here are some possible questions:

- A good reader "reads between the lines." What inferences do you make about Shakira's feelings about her mother's choice of activities for her? How about the boy, her brother? How do you think their father feels about the Michael's activity? Why did the author include this section in the article?

- On page 7, the author states, *Shakira was lucky.* In what ways was Shakira lucky? In what ways was Shakira unlucky?

Extend the reading. Here are some additional activities to expand students' understanding:

- Students may enjoy reading the article as if they are radio announcers or newscasters. Role-playing is likely to make the readers feel more at ease and less self-conscious reading aloud. You could even provide a microphone as a prop.

- *For English Language Learners* Guide students to the first and second paragraphs under the heading "Table for Four, Please." Model for students how to highlight all of the words that end in -er. (*quicker, easier, healthier*) Explain that these words mean "more quickly," "more easily," and "more healthily." Explain that the comparative of most one-syllable adjectives is formed by adding -er. Show students how to change the y at the end of an adjective to an *i* before adding -er. (*funny* becomes *funnier, easy* becomes *easier.*) Explain that words with three or more syllables (*beautiful, intelligent*) are formed by adding "more" before them (*more beautiful, more intelligent.*)

- Have students work in pairs or small groups to choose one of the following situations: A) The family is eating dinner at a fast food restaurant; B) The parent is choosing a treat for dessert at home; C) The parent is choosing a beverage for the child. Have students work together to find a main idea from the text that relates to their scenario. Then students fill out a main idea and supporting details graphic organizer. You may wish to model this strategy. For example, a group might choose situation A. Their main idea might be, *Encourage a child to choose one of the healthier meals on the menu.* Their supporting details might be, *1. Most fast food meals are unhealthy; 2. Unhealthy eating can lead to weight gain and health problems; 3. Many fast food restaurants have options that are healthier than burgers and fries.*

- At home, have each student find an article in a newspaper or magazine about weight or other health problems, particularly for children. Tell them to read the article, bring it to class, and to prepare a graphic organizer that shows the main ideas and details from that article.

Use reading skills: Identify main idea and details. Experienced readers know that identifying the main idea and details is critical to understanding works of nonfiction. It is an important part of the text structure, the way that the author organizes the article. Point out to students that often there is a main idea for the whole piece of text, and usually a main idea for each paragraph. The details support the main ideas.

Use a graphic organizer. The main idea/supporting details chart visually organizes how the details support the argument the writer is making. In this case the main idea tells how much exercise a child needs each day. The details may expand on this idea by naming some of the activities a child may do in order to maintain a good weight. The chart helps the reader organize the writer's ideas.

Write About It (PAGES 13–14)

Write an explanation. Have students read the directions on page 13. Be sure they understand that they will write a paragraph in response to a friend's letter asking for advice to help her overweight son lose weight.

Prewriting Remind students that there are different ways to respond to the friend's letter. Some solutions can come from the article they have just read, and some solutions can come from what they know from experience. Model for students how to fill in the graphic organizer, and encourage them to find additional details. Tell them to choose the strongest argument as the basis for the paragraph.

Thinking Beyond Reading Have students work with a partner or a small group to discuss the questions. The intent is for students to probe more deeply and to elaborate

on the topic by addressing issues that did not arise when they were first thinking about childhood obesity and what parents can do to change children's lifestyles. Encourage them to add ideas to their graphic organizers.

Write a draft. Have students write independently. Write on the board this sample topic sentence: *Parents can help a heavy child lose weight.* Be sure that students understand that all the sentences in the paragraph must relate to the same main idea, in this case how a parent can help a child lose weight. Remind students to use the details in their graphic organizers to organize the different elements of their responses. While drafting, students should not be concerned with spelling or punctuation. Encourage them to write their thoughts quickly and freely.

Revise and create a final draft. Remind students to use the Revising and Editing Checklist (Master 11) to guide them in revising their writing. Have students review each other's writing and give each other feedback on the parts of the paragraph that are logical, clear, interesting, and convincing, and the parts that need revision.

When students have finished revising their writing, use the Writing Rubric (Master 10) to evaluate it. Be sure you review your response with each student so he or she understands the strengths and weaknesses of this piece of writing. Have students date the writing and put the completed pieces in their writing portfolios.

Building Fluency

Identify small sections from "Goodbye Cookies, Hello Apples." Tell students that they will use echo reading to read these sections aloud. Put students into groups of two. Give them time to read a passage silently 2–3 times to encourage their best oral reading. Remind them to pay attention to words that cause them to stumble. They will imitate your phrasing and intonation for each sentence. Remind students to use punctuation and typographic cues to add expression to their reading. Tell them that the goal is to read the passage as fluently as if they were just speaking.

Growing Your Job Possibilities

Lesson Overview: (PAGE 15)

Theme

Have students read the lesson title on page 15 and tell them that the title introduces the lesson theme, Work. Discuss the theme by having students share what kind of work they do now or have done in the past. Encourage students to share what they do or do not enjoy about their work.

Learning Objectives

Be sure students understand the outcome of each of the learning goals.

- *Read a story about one man's job at a plant nursery. Point out that this is fiction, but it deals with a real issue of how a person's interests and values can shape his or her career path.*
- *Learn to recognize cause and effect.*
- *Master the key vocabulary used in the story.*
- *Write a description of how to grow healthy roses.*

Preteach the vocabulary. (PAGE 15)

Read the key vocabulary words and their definitions to the students. Tell them that they will recognize all these words in the story.

- Distribute the Vocabulary Knowledge Rating Chart (Master 9) and have students individually rate each of the key vocabulary words.
- Review particularly challenging words with students by listing each one on the board, modeling its use in a sentence, and having two or three students use the word in original sentences. Reframe student sentences that do not use the new words correctly.

You may wish to offer a mini-lesson on adjectives as students read the respective parts of speech with the definitions of the vocabulary words. [See page 41 of this book for a mini-lesson on adjectives. Use Master 5 or 6 to give students practice in recognizing adjectives.]

Before You Read (PAGE 16)

In the course of reading this story, students will be learning about a relationship between two people, about taking care of roses, and about how someone decides on a career. Explain that using what they already know about one or all of these things will help them understand the story. Tell them also that good readers visualize the characters and action in a story to help them follow what is happening. Encourage them to visualize as they read the story.

As students begin to write answers to the questions for each element on page 16, have them read the respective Think About Its in the side column.

Use what you know. Use the first Think About It about growing tomatoes to encourage students to talk about their own successes and challenges with gardening. Students may also wish to explore their opinions about working for money versus working for passion.

Visualize as you read. Have students read the first four paragraphs of the story and the second Think About It. You may wish to have students close their eyes and concentrate as a partner reads the paragraphs aloud. Have the listeners describe each detail of what they "saw" in their minds as the story was being read. Which senses were stimulated as they visualized the scene? Responses might include sight, sound, and smell.

Reading the Story (PAGES 17–19)

Emphasize to students that reading to find out about Gil's relationship with his father gives them a purpose for reading the passage. Suggest that highlighting phrases that show how their mutual interest brought the father and son closer will help keep students involved in the story.

Side-Column Vocabulary Remind students that the vocabulary words and phrases in the side column have been selected as important to the theme and content of the story. These words may be useful in the context of business and corporations, but may not be part of everyday language.

Mid-Passage Questions   Some of the answers to the questions call on students' judgments, so there are not many right or wrong answers. Review students' written answers to assess whether they are getting meaning from the text. They should indicate in their answers what took place in the story that helped Gil develop his interests, his relationship with his father, and his later re-evaluation of his life. Ask students to comment on how realistic they think these events and characters are.

After You Read (PAGES 20–22)

Build a robust vocabulary.   Ask students to check their answers in the answer keys in their books.

Think about your reading.   Ask students to check their answers in the answer keys in their books. Ask additional questions to enrich the discussion so that students will be better able to write descriptions. Here are some possible questions:

- A good reader looks for cause and effect relationships. What was the cause of Gil's love of gardening? How did Maria affect Gil's career path when they were teenagers? What was the effect of Gil's family needing more money than Gil was earning as a manager? What was the effect of Gil's father's death on Gil? Have students find sentences in the story that support their answers.

- How do you know that Gil was satisfied with his decision to retire?

   Extend the reading.   Here are some additional activities to expand students' understanding.

   - Students may enjoy practicing the parts and then dramatizing a dialogue from the text. Gil's and Papa's conversation at the beginning of the story offers the opportunity for pairs of students to perform in front of small groups or the entire class.

   - *For English Language Learners*   Have students take turns drawing a scene from "For a Love of Roses." Have a partner describe the illustration with as much detail as possible. Encourage students to use prepositions such as *in, on, next to, beneath,* and *above* when describing the

drawings. Tell students not to be concerned with the quality of their drawings.

- Model for students an example of a sentence that includes many sensory details. (*I felt the softness of the yellow petals tickle my nose as I inhaled their sweet perfume.*) Work with students to determine how many senses were used. Encourage pairs of students to create and share their own multi-sensory sentences.

- At home, have each student find a radio or television advertisement that refers to several senses. Have students write and share with the class a detailed description of the ad, including how many senses the advertisement required the listener or viewer to use.

Use reading skills: Recognize cause and effect. Experienced readers of narrative fiction know that for every action in a text, there is a cause or motivation. Characters, just like real people, have reasons for acting the way they do. Remind students that their own life experiences will affect how they respond to the characters. What has caused students to make the life choices that they have made? Were there influential people who gave them advice? Was the effect of the advice positive or negative?

Use a graphic organizer.   The cause and effect chart in this lesson shows that one event in the story has several causes. It provides a visual way to organize this information.

Write About It (PAGES 23–24)

Write a description.   Have students read the directions on page 23 and be sure they understand that they will write a paragraph that tells how to raise healthy rose bushes.

Prewriting   Remind students that effective descriptive writing appeals to the senses and allows the reader to visualize the situation. While reading "For a Love of Roses," students have learned about caring for roses. In this activity, students will use that knowledge to respond to a letter and describe how to care for roses properly. The graphic organizer will help students organize their ideas and ensure that they are providing an answer for every question in the letter.

Thinking Beyond Reading   Have students work with a partner or a small group to discuss the questions. The intent is for students to probe more deeply and to elaborate on the topic by addressing issues that did not arise when they were first thinking about growing roses. Encourage them to add ideas to their charts.

Write a draft.   Have students write independently. Be sure that students understand that they must respond to all of the questions and situations posed in the letter. In addition, students are to explain the proper way to care for rose bushes. Encourage students to use descriptive words, including, if possible, the vocabulary from the story (*fragrant, maintenance,* and *luscious*). While drafting, students should not be concerned with spelling or punctuation. Encourage them to write their thoughts quickly and freely.

Revise and create a final draft.   Remind students to use the Revising and Editing Checklist (Master 11) to guide them in revising their writing. Have students review each other's writing and give each other feedback on the parts of the paragraph that are logical, clear, and interesting, and the parts that need revision.

When students have finished revising their writing, use the Writing Rubric (Master 10) to evaluate their writing. Be sure you review your response with each student so he or she understands the strengths and weaknesses of this piece of writing. Have students date the writing and put the completed pieces in their writing portfolios.

Building Fluency

Identify small sections from "For a Love of Roses." Tell students that they will use paired reading to read these sections aloud. Put students into groups of two. Give them time to read a passage silently 2–3 times to encourage their best oral reading. Partners take turns being the reader or listener. After the first reading, the listener does not provide feedback. After the second and third readings, the listener provides feedback to the reader. Remind students to pay attention to words that cause them to stumble and to read for the author's message. Their goal is to read the passage as fluently as if they were just speaking.

A New Kind of Family

Lesson Overview: (PAGE 25)

Theme

Have students read the lesson title on page 25, and tell them that the title introduces the lesson theme, Family. Discuss the theme by inviting students to make personal connections, telling who raised them and with whom they live now. Have students share if they know of any families in which grandparents are raising their grandchildren.

Learning objectives

Be sure students understand the outcome of each of the learning goals.

- *Learn about grandfamilies.* Provide background about the article by explaining that it is nonfiction and contains information about grandparents raising grandchildren.

- *Learn to classify ideas into categories.*

- *Master the key vocabulary used in the article.*

- *Write an e-mail to a friend.*

Preteach the vocabulary. (PAGE 26)

Read the key vocabulary words and their definitions to the students. Tell them that they will recognize all these words in the article.

- Distribute the Vocabulary Knowledge Rating Chart (Master 9) and have students individually rate each of the key vocabulary words.

- Review particularly challenging words with students by listing each one on the board, modeling its use in a sentence, and having two or three students use the word in original sentences. Reframe student sentences that do not use the new words correctly.

You may wish to offer a mini-lesson on nouns as students read the respective parts of speech with the definitions of the vocabulary words. [See page 39 in this book for a mini-lesson on nouns. Use Master 1 or 2 to give students practice in recognizing nouns.]

Before You Read (PAGE 26)

Help students to understand that good readers ask themselves questions before, during, and after reading. Before reading, good readers read the title, look at any illustrations, and scan the text and headings. They ask themselves questions about what they might learn from the text. During reading, good readers continue to form questions based on the text. They also look for the answers to the questions they have already asked. After reading, good readers ask themselves if the questions they asked have been answered, and what those answers are. If the questions have not been answered, good readers look further for answers.

As students begin to write answers to the questions for each element on page 26, have them read the respective Think About Its.

Use what you know. Use the first Think About It to discuss students' experiences and relationships with grandparents. In answering the questions, students' experiences are likely to vary considerably, from never having known their grandparents to having been raised by grandparents. If there is not time to hear from each student, you may wish to have students pair off and share their experiences with one another.

Ask yourself questions. Have students answer the questions on page 26. Invite them to share their answers and the special experience between a grandparent and grandchild that they have written about. Explain to students that by getting them invested in their questions and answers, you are encouraging them to read the article carefully. Generally, students will ask questions of themselves as readers and look for the answers themselves.

Reading the Article (PAGES 27–29)

Emphasize to students that reading to find out what a grandfamily is gives them a purpose for reading the article. It is a question to answer as they read. Encourage students to write questions on sticky notes as a strategy for keeping track of the questions that come up while they are reading. Remind them that it is always valuable to circle words that they do not know as they read. They should list these words in their personal dictionaries so they can learn them.

Side-Column Vocabulary Remind students that the vocabulary words and phrases in the side column have been selected as important to the theme and content of the article. These words may be useful in the context of families and their interactions with social services, but they are not necessarily part of everyday language.

Mid-Passage Questions The answers to the questions call on students' judgments, so there are no right or wrong answers. Review students' written answers to assess whether they are getting meaning from the text. They should indicate in their answers that grandparents and grandchildren may have different feelings about grandfamilies.

After You Read (PAGES 30–32)

Build a robust vocabulary. Ask students to check their answers in the answer keys in their books.

Think about your reading. Ask students to check their answers in the answer keys in their books. Ask additional questions to enrich the discussion so that students will be better able to write about family issues. Here are some possible questions:

- Good readers ask questions of themselves and the text. Ask students what question they asked themselves when they read the first sentence of the second paragraph under the heading "Knock, Knock." Students might respond that there seem to be two kinds of parents in grandfamilies—parents who want to take care of their children, but can't; and parents who do not wish to take care of their children.

- In this text, the author asks the reader questions after the title and after the heading "What About Me?" Ask students what purpose these questions at the beginning of a section serve. Students might say that the questions help them to focus on the information the section is about to provide.

Extend the reading. Here are some additional activities to expand students' understanding:

- Students may enjoy working in small groups to dramatize the reasons that grandparents end up raising their grandchildren. You may wish to write some of the reasons (drugs, untimely death, illness, parents looking for work, violence in the home, parent in jail) on slips of paper. Have each small group write and perform a short skit dramatizing one of those reasons.

- *For English Language Learners* Tell students that there are many compound words in English, words that combine two words into one word. Ask students if compound words exist in their native language; if so, have students share examples. Show students some examples of compound words in "Grandma, I'm Home!" (Examples: *grandparent, homework, downtown*) Identify with students the two words in each compound word, and define the word when the words are put together. Have students find and share additional compound words from the article (*grandfamily, everyday*) or elsewhere.

- Have students work in small groups to share and discuss the questions they wrote on their sticky notes as they were reading. Did they find the answers in the text? What questions remained? What questions did different readers have in common? What questions were unique to particular readers? Have the groups share their findings with the class.

- At home, have each student interview two people from different families about their relationships with a grandparent. Encourage students to write their questions beforehand, and have students write a paragraph summary of each interview to share in small groups. You may wish to model examples of questions:

Did/do you have a special relationship with one of your grandparents? Do you have a particular, special memory of that grandparent?

Use reading skills: Classify information. Explain to students that when we classify, we sort things into groups of ideas or things that go together. By classifying (or organizing) ideas in our reading by what they have in common, we can remember them more easily. Some students will say that we classify things in our everyday lives. One example might be the grocery store. Usually, stores are organized so the produce is in one place, the meat is in another place, and bread is in its own aisle. The items in each of those sections have something in common.

Use a graphic organizer. In this lesson, the chart helps organize the ideas that relate to a common theme, Reasons Why Grandparents Raise Grandchildren. The graphic organizer can help students analyze narrative or informative text in order to understand it better. It can also serve as a planning tool to organize a writer's thinking about the text.

Write About It (PAGES 33–34)

Write an e-mail. Have students read the directions at the top of page 33. Be sure they understand that they will write an e-mail explaining how they feel about having a grandchild living with them.

Prewriting Show students how to use the chart to organize their writing. Students can work in pairs to think of the information they would like to include in their e-mails. This will help them write the e-mails in an organized manner, so sentences follow each other logically and they present their cases clearly.

Thinking Beyond Reading Have students work with a partner or a small group to discuss the questions. The intent is for students to probe more deeply and to elaborate on the topic by addressing issues that did not arise when they were first thinking about grandfamilies. Encourage

them to add ideas to their charts. The more organized their charts are, the more easily students will be able to organize their writing.

Write a draft. Have students write independently. Write on the board the following topic sentences: *I want my grandchild to live with me. I don't want my grandchild to live with me.* Be sure that students understand that all the sentences in their e-mails must relate to the main idea they have chosen. Remind students to use the ideas in their charts to organize the different elements of their responses. These ideas will be the details in their paragraphs. While drafting, students should not be concerned with spelling or punctuation. Encourage them to write their thoughts quickly and freely.

Revise and create a final draft. Remind students to use the Revising and Editing Checklist (Master 11) to guide them in revising their writing. Have students review each other's writing and give each other feedback on the parts of the e-mail that are logical, clear, and interesting, and the parts that need revision.

When students have finished revising their writing, use the Writing Rubric (Master 10) to evaluate it. Be sure you review your response with each student so he or she understands the strengths and weaknesses of this piece of writing. Have students date the writing and put the completed pieces in their writing portfolios.

Building Fluency

Identify small sections from "Grandma, I'm Home!" Tell students that they will use paired reading to read these sections aloud. Put students into groups of two. Give them time to read a passage silently 2–3 times to encourage their best oral reading. Partners take turns being the reader or listener. After the first reading, the listener does not provide feedback. After the second and third readings, the listener provides feedback to the reader. Remind students to pay attention to words that cause them to stumble and to read for the author's message. Their goal is to read the passage as fluently as if they were just speaking.

Friends and Neighbors

Lesson Overview: (PAGE 35)

Theme

Have students read the lesson title on page 35 and tell them that the title introduces the lesson theme, Community. Discuss the theme by having students make personal connections, describing the communities they grew up in or where they live now. Do they know many of their neighbors? Do they tend to buy what they need in big stores or in little shops?

Learning objectives

Be sure students understand the outcome of each of the learning goals.

- *Read a story about a young man and a small store in a crisis.* Point out that this story is fiction, but it tells about how important friends and neighbors can be in a real crisis.
- *Learn to identify cause and effect.*
- *Master the key vocabulary used in the story.*
- *Write a summary paragraph that tells what happens in the story.*

Preteach the vocabulary. (PAGE 35)

Read the key vocabulary words and their definitions to students. Tell them that they will recognize all these words in the story.

- Distribute the Vocabulary Knowledge Rating Chart (Master 9) and have students individually rate each of the key vocabulary words.
- Review particularly challenging words with students by listing each one on the board, modeling its use in a sentence, and having two or three students use the word in original sentences. Reframe student sentences that do not use the new words correctly.

You may wish to offer a mini-lesson on adverbs as students read the respective parts of speech with the definitions of the vocabulary words. [See page 42 of this book for a mini-lesson on adverbs. Use Master 7 or 8 to give students practice in recognizing adverbs.]

Before You Read (PAGE 36)

Explain that good readers respond to the ideas on the page. One way to respond is by asking and answering questions as they read. Encourage students to use sticky notes to write questions and highlighters to indicate the answers to those questions.

As students begin to write answers to the questions for each element on page 36, have them read the respective Think About Its.

Make predictions about the story. Have students discuss how the title, "After the Storm," suggests that something will probably happens that will "shake up" Jesse's life. Whether it will be a literal or a figurative "storm" is something that the reader might consider. Use the first Think About It to elicit discussion about how unexpected events can completely change things. Students may tell about events in their own lives or recall other stories in which a character suddenly has something exciting happen to change his or her life.

Visualize as you read. Have students read the first paragraph of "After the Storm" and then read the second Think About It. Ask students what they visualize the rest of the downtown area looks like. What do they see, smell, and hear? By picturing the scene in their heads, good readers have more information with which to understand the text and predict events in the passage.

Reading the Story (PAGES 37–39)

Emphasize to students that they will read to find out what is bothering Jesse. This gives them a purpose for reading the story. It is a question to answer as they read. Highlighting phrases that are clues to Jesse's problem is a strategy that will keep them involved in the story.

Side-Column Vocabulary   Remind students that the vocabulary words and phrases in the side column have been selected as important to the theme and content of the story. These words may be useful in the context of retelling, but they are not necessarily part of everyday language.

Mid-Passage Questions   The answers to the questions call on students' judgments, so there are no right or wrong answers. Review students' written answers to assess whether they are getting meaning from the text. Ask them to share how they thought the storm would affect the relationship between Jesse and his father. Finally, ask students if they predicted the ending of the story correctly and if they believe Jesse will continue to be content in his community.

After You Read (PAGES 40–42)

Build a robust vocabulary.   Ask students to check their answers in the answer keys in their books.

Think about your reading.   Ask students to check their answers in the answer keys in their books. Ask additional questions to enrich the discussion so that students will be better able to write about Jesse's problem. Here are some possible questions:

- In "After the Storm," the author provides descriptions of Jesse's body language. What does the following description tell you about Jesse's feelings or attitudes: "Jesse sighed, slipped on his jacket, and walked silently home with his dad"? What other examples of body language in the story create vivid images and tell you about the characters' feelings or attitudes?

- The author uses the word *maybe* three times in the last three sentences. What was the author's reason for repeating that word?

Extend the reading.   Here are some additional activities to expand students' understanding.

- Students may enjoy taking parts and reading the dialogues aloud. The conversation between Jesse and Mrs. Aguirro on p. 37 and the exchange on p. 39 when the neighbors come

to help clean provide good opportunities for oral reading. Encourage students to read with as much natural expression as they can.

- *For English Language Learners* Transition words tie one sentence to the next sentence in a paragraph. Words such as *also, furthermore,* and *moreover* continue a common line of reasoning. Words such as *however, nevertheless,* and *yet* contrast ideas. Transition words can make writing and speaking clearer and more exact. Have students practice tying sentences together using transition words. Use these examples: "Jesse felt stuck in is life. He found his work at the store boring." (*Also, Furthermore,* or *Moreover*) "The policemen and firemen worked hard to keep the water contained. The river flooded the stores downtown." (*However, Nevertheless,* or *Yet*) Have students write more sentences using transition words.

- Invite students to play a cause/effect game in groups of three. For each round, each student chooses one of three cards—*event, cause,* or *effect.* The student who chooses *event* states an event that happened in "After the Storm." The person with *cause* states a cause of the event. The person with *effect* states an effect of the event. The group decides together if they have earned a point for that round. You may wish to model a round. The event might be: "Jesse's father swept the front walk." A cause of sweeping might be: "People littered on the sidewalk." An effect of sweeping might be: "Jesse's father then felt ready to head home for the day."

- At home, have students draw maps of their communities, labeling the places they frequent. You may wish to have students present their community maps to small groups or to the class, and have them share what they like or dislike about the communities in which they live.

Use reading skills: Identify cause and effect. Experienced readers of fiction know that for every action in a text there is a cause or motivation. Characters, just like real people, have reasons for acting the way they act, and events are affected by prior events. When they connect causes to their effects, good readers understand the characters and the plot more clearly. By understanding cause and effect, readers can also predict more accurately what will happen as the story continues.

Use a graphic organizer. The chart for this lesson helps the reader see cause and effect relationships. It shows visually that if you know a cause you can look for its effect and if you know an effect you can look for its cause.

Write About It (PAGES 43–44)

Write a story summary. Have students read the directions on page 43. Be sure they understand that they will write a paragraph summarizing the main events in "After the Storm."

Prewriting Remind students that a summary takes the important events in a story and condenses them into one clear paragraph. In order to write a summary, students must first determine what the important events were in "After the Storm." Students will use the main events from the graphic organizer as their sentences.

Thinking Beyond Reading Have students work with a partner or a small group to discuss the questions. The intent is for students to probe more deeply and to think carefully about what to include in their summaries. Encourage them to think about which ideas are the most important.

Write a draft. Have students write independently. Be sure that students understand that each of the sentences

in the paragraph should describe an important event from the story. While drafting, students should not be concerned with spelling or punctuation. Encourage them to write their thoughts quickly and freely.

Revise and create a final draft. Remind students to use the Revising and Editing Checklist (Master 11) to guide them in revising their writing. Have students review each other's writing and give each other feedback on the parts of the paragraph that are logical, clear, and interesting, and the parts that need revision.

When students have finished revising their writing, use the Writing Rubric (Master 10) to evaluate it. Be sure you review your response with each student so he or she understands the strengths and weaknesses of this piece of writing. Have students date the writing and put the completed pieces in their writing portfolios.

Building Fluency

Identify small sections from "After the Storm." Tell students that they will use paired reading to read these sections aloud. Put students into groups of two. Give them time to read a passage silently 2–3 times to encourage their best oral reading. Partners take turns being the reader or listener. After the first reading, the listener does not provide feedback. After the second and third readings, the listener provides feedback to the reader. Remind students to pay attention to words that cause them to stumble and to read for the author's message. Their goal is to read the passage as fluently as if they were just speaking.

Read All About It

Lesson Overview: (PAGE 45)

Theme

Have students read the lesson title on page 45 and tell them that the title introduces the lesson theme, School and Education. Discuss the theme by having students make personal connections, sharing their overall impressions of their schooling. Have students tell whether they faced any particular challenges in school, such as difficulty with a particular teacher or a struggle with a particular subject.

Learning objectives

Be sure students understand the outcome of each of the learning goals.

- *Read about a man who learned to read as an adult.* Explain that this article is nonfiction. It gives accurate information about a man who couldn't read, an issue that is important in many people's lives.

- *Learn to identify words that show time order.*

- *Master the key vocabulary used in the article.*

- *Write directions telling a child how to get ready for school.*

Preteach the vocabulary. (PAGE 45)

Read the key vocabulary words and their definitions to the students. Tell them that they will recognize all these words in the article.

- Distribute the Vocabulary Knowledge Rating Chart (Master 9) and have students individually rate each of the key vocabulary words.

- Review particularly challenging words with students by listing each one on the board, modeling its use in a sentence, and having two or three students use the word in original sentences. Reframe student sentences that do not use the new words correctly.

You may wish to offer a mini-lesson on verbs as students read the respective parts of speech with the definitions of the vocabulary words. [See page 40 of this book for a mini-lesson on verbs. Use Master 3 or 4 to give students practice in recognizing verbs.]

Before You Read (PAGE 46)

Explain that good readers pick and choose among a variety of strategies. They use strategies that will most effectively help them understand the particular text they are reading. Encourage students to have a pen and/or highlighter and sticky notes on hand no matter what they are reading. For this article, students will want to keep track of the order of events in the main character's life. They may wish to highlight the words that indicate when events took place. They may also wish to use sticky notes to record the questions that they have as they read.

As students begin to write answers to the questions for each element on page 46, have them read the respective Think About Its.

Use what you know. Use the Think About It to elicit background knowledge from students. Have students share what problems they or someone they know has had in school and what solutions they found for those problems. Would students do things differently if they could? How might students help other people (such as their children, and nieces or nephews) if they saw those youngsters facing similar problems? Remind students that using the knowledge that they have will help them have a deeper understanding of the article they are about to read.

Make predictions while you read. Have students read the first section of "It's Never too Late" and then read the Think About It. Ask students if they think that John's fear of the teasing may keep him from telling anyone that he cannot read and getting help with his problem. Have students predict what strategies John will use to succeed in life without being able to read. Suggest that students jot down their predictions before they continue reading and then check to see if their predictions are correct.

Reading the Article (PAGES 47–49)

Emphasize to students that they should read to find out how John got by in school. It is a question to answer as they read. Highlighting phrases that are clues to how John maintained his secret is a strategy that will keep them involved in the article.

Side-Column Vocabulary Remind students that the vocabulary words and phrases in the side column have been selected as important to the theme and content of the story. These words may be useful in the context of school and work, but they are not necessarily part of everyday language.

Mid-Passage Questions Some of the answers to the questions call on students' judgments, so there are not many right or wrong answers. Review students' written answers to assess whether they are getting meaning from the text. They should indicate in their answers that John first admitted that he couldn't read when he was 48, and it was surprising because he was so successful. Students should also indicate that John's "bruises" were emotional scars and humiliation.

After You Read (PAGES 50–51)

Build a robust vocabulary. Ask students to check their answers in the answer keys in their books.

Think about your reading. Ask students to check their answers in the answer keys in their books. Ask additional questions to enrich the discussion so that students will be better able to write about the events in John's life. Here are some possible questions:

- A good reader follows the events in the text carefully. What was the turning point in John's life—when did he decide to ask for help? Why was it so difficult for John to admit that he was illiterate?

- Do you think John could have gone his whole life without learning to read? How did learning to read change John's life?

    Extend the reading. Here are some additional activities to expand students' understanding:

- Students may enjoy reading the article as if they are newscasters telling a story. The first section of "It's Never too Late" is ideal for this type of Reader's Theater and may help to build fluency. Have students take turns with the role—speaking as if they are someone else. Be sure to give students ample time to practice reading before they perform.

- *For English Language Learners* Have students work with the following time order words: *first, next, then, after that, finally.* Have each student choose a simple skill that can be broken into about five steps (for example, making a sandwich, washing a car, putting a child to sleep). Have students practice with a partner explaining the steps involved in the task. Then have students present the steps to the class. Make sure that students are using the time order words appropriately. You may wish to model this activity.

- Make copies of the article. Cut the article into one- or two-paragraph sections, and give pairs of students the cut-up article. Have students put the article back in order without looking at the original text. Have students share what clues they used to piece the story back together and what pieces were particularly challenging.

- At home, have each student find an article in a newspaper or magazine that tells a story in chronological order. Have students read the article and then cut the article into one or two paragraph sections. In class, give the cut-up articles to small groups to piece back together. Remind them to be aware of time order words if they are used in the article.

Use reading skills: Identify time order. Experienced readers know that not all stories are written in the exact order the events occurred. Sometimes, the author jumps around in time to best tell the story. Ask students why the author of "It's Never too Late" gave an overview and then told the story from the beginning to give more detail. Have students scan the article and identify the time order words at the start of various paragraphs.

Use a graphic organizer. The time order chart in this lesson helps the reader get a clearer sense of the order of events. It visually organizes the events and helps students analyze the importance of the information.

Write About It (PAGES 53–54)

Write directions. Have students read the directions on page 53. Be sure they understand that they will write directions to help a seven-year-old boy get ready for school on time.

Prewriting Remind students that seven-year-olds require specific directions. In the case of this particular seven-year-old, time management seems to be an issue. Students should first think of all of the things involved in getting ready for school. Then, they should order the activities so the boy will be able to follow the directions to get ready in a timely manner. You may wish to have students write their ideas on sticky notes and rearrange/order the sticky notes prior to filling out the chart.

Thinking Beyond Reading Have students work with a partner or a small group discuss the questions. The intent is for students to probe more deeply and to elaborate on the topic by addressing issues that did not arise when they were first thinking about helping a child get ready for school in the morning. Encourage them to add ideas to their charts.

Write a draft. Have students write independently. Write on the board the following topic sentence: *It is important for a child to get to school on time.* Be sure that students understand that all the sentences in the paragraph must relate to the same main idea, in this case how to get ready for school in a timely manner. Remind students to use their charts to organize the steps. They will also need to choose appropriate time order words. You may wish to model for students the use of words such as *first, second, then, later, before, after,* and *finally.* While drafting, students should not be concerned with spelling or punctuation. Encourage them to write their thoughts quickly and freely.

Revise and create a final draft. Remind students to use the Revising and Editing Checklist (Master 11) to guide them in revising their writing. Have students review each other's writing and give each other feedback on the parts of the paragraph that are logical, clear, and appropriate for a seven-year-old, and the parts that need revision.

When students have finished revising their writing, use the Writing Rubric (Master 10) to evaluate it. Be sure you review your response with each student so he or she understands the strengths and weaknesses of this piece of writing. Have students date the writing and put the completed pieces in their writing portfolios.

Building Fluency

Identify small sections from "It's Never too Late." Tell students that they will use choral reading to read these sections aloud. (See page 7 of this book for a description of choral reading.) Give them time to read a passage silently 2–3 times to encourage the best oral reading. In order to set and maintain the pace, read along with the students. Identify words that cause the students to stumble. They will imitate the phrasing and intonation that you model. Remind students to use punctuation and typographic cues to add expression to their reading. Tell them that the goal is to read the passage as fluently as if they were just speaking.

Hard Work Pays Off

Lesson Overview: (PAGE 55)

Theme

Have students read the lesson title on page 55 and tell them that the title introduces the lesson theme, Civics and Government. Discuss the theme by having students make personal connections, sharing experiences they have had with government or politicians. Ask students whether they vote in elections. Why or why not?

Learning Objectives

Be sure students understand the outcome of each of the learning goals.

- *Learn about a Congresswoman from Florida.* Tell students that this is a true story about some events in the life of Ileana Ros-Lehtinen, a member of Congress who represents a district in South Florida.
- *Learn to make judgments about information.*
- *Master the key vocabulary used in the article.*
- *Write a letter to the editor.*

Preteach the vocabulary. (PAGE 55)

Read the key vocabulary words and their definitions to the students. Tell them that they will recognize all these words in the article.

- Distribute the Vocabulary Knowledge Rating Chart (Master 9) and have students individually rate each of the key vocabulary words.
- Review particularly challenging words with students by listing each one on the board, modeling its use in a sentence, and having two or three students use the word in original sentences. Reframe student sentences that do not use the new words correctly.

You may wish to offer a mini-lesson on nouns as students read the respective parts of speech with the definitions of the vocabulary words. [See page 39 of this book for a mini-lesson on nouns. Use Master 1 or 2 to give students practice in recognizing nouns.]

Before You Read (PAGE 56)

Explain that effective readers react to what they read. They get involved and therefore remember more. Involved readers make judgments as they read. Do they agree with the beliefs and opinions of the subject of the article? Do they share the author's respect or dislike of the subject? Seeing if those judgments still hold true after reading the entire article can keep a reader interested throughout.

As students begin to write answers to the questions for each element on page 56, have them read the respective Think About Its in the side column.

Use what you know. Use the Think About It to elicit discussion about non-English speakers' experiences adapting to life in the United States. Do students or people they know have a first language other than English? What particular challenges do non-English speakers face in American schools?

Preview the article. Help students figure out from the title that "Hola, Congresswoman!" is about a congresswoman who speaks Spanish. Students may infer that she is originally from another country. As students preview the headings in the article they will see that the article also includes information about the job of a U.S. legislator.

Reading the Story (PAGES 57–59)

Emphasize to students that reading to find out about how a non-English speaking Hispanic woman became a successful Congresswoman from Florida gives them a purpose for reading the passage. Suggest that they use a highlighter to keep track of her actions, and that they make notes in the margins with their own opinions. These two strategies will keep them involved in the article.

Side-Column Vocabulary Remind students that the vocabulary words and phrases in the side column have been selected as important to the theme and content of the story. These words may be useful in the context of government and legislation, but they are not necessarily part of everyday language.

Mid-Passage Questions Some of the answers to the questions call on students' judgments, so there are not many right or wrong answers. Review students' written answers to assess whether they are getting meaning from the text. They should indicate in their answers that the Congresswoman is persistent and fights for women's rights and the environment. Ask students if they think her background as a teacher has been important in her career.

After You Read (PAGES 60–61)

Build a robust vocabulary. Ask students to check their answers in the answer keys in their books.

Think about your reading. Ask students to check their answers in the answer keys in their books. Ask additional questions to enrich the discussion so that students will be better able to write about the Congresswoman's effectiveness. Here are some possible questions.

- The author says that Congresswoman Ros-Lehtinen quickly learned English when she arrived in the United States from Cuba. Why do you think she was determined to learn English quickly? How might the Congresswoman's life have been different if she had not learned English? Do you believe that all immigrants to the United States should learn English? Why or why not?

- From your own judgment, does Congresswoman Ros-Lehtinen work more toward her own goals or toward the goals of her constituents? How does the text support your response?

Extend the reading. Here are some additional activities to expand students' understanding.

- Have groups of 5–8 students each write a summary of the article. Have the first student

write a sentence on a piece of paper and then pass the paper to his or her left. Continue with each student adding a sentence that tells what happened next in Ros-Lehtinen's life. When everyone has added a sentence, the last student in the group reads the summary.

- *For English Language Learners* Explain that being able to identify the roots of words gives students access to a number of different words that include that root. Remind students that there are a number of prefixes in English that mean *not* (*mis-, dis-, in-, non-, im-*) and a few suffixes that turn a verb into its corresponding noun form (*-tion, -sion, -ment*). Use the following roots from the article as the basis for practice with roots and affixes: *judge* (misjudge, judgment); *able* (ability, disable); *educate* (education, uneducated).

- At home, have students learn as much as they can about their congressional district and representative. Have students write what they learn and share at least three interesting facts with the class.

Use reading skills: Make judgments. Explain to students that a judgment is an opinion based on information combined with life experiences. As readers, they make judgments about the beliefs and opinions of the author, such as their regard for the congresswoman's character. Remind students that although the judgments are the opinions of the readers, those readers should be able to support their judgments with information from the text.

Use a graphic organizer. This chart visually organizes the elements that go into making a judgment. It helps a reader to put information from the article together with his or her background knowledge to arrive at a judgment.

Write About It (PAGES 63–64)

Write a letter to the editor. Have students read the directions on page 63. Be sure they understand that they will write a letter to the editor telling whether they support the construction of a cement plant.

Prewriting Remind students that a letter to the editor must be short and to the point. Encourage them to use the information and opinions from the editorial on page 63 in combination with what they know and believe in order to fill in the graphic organizer. How will they combine facts with opinions in order to make their own judgments about the cement plant? Then how will they write their letters to persuade other people to agree with their judgments? They must write in convincing sentences, but caution them against getting emotional.

Thinking Beyond Reading Have students work with a partner or a small group to discuss the questions. The intent is for students to probe more deeply and to elaborate on the topic by addressing issues that did not arise when they were first considering a new cement plant in their neighborhood. Encourage them to add ideas to their charts.

Write a draft. Have students write independently. Students will need to decide which side of this issue they will support. Be sure that students understand that all the sentences in the paragraph must relate to the same main idea, in this case whether or not the cement plant is a good plan. Remind students to use the points they made in their charts to organize their responses. While drafting, students should not be concerned with spelling or punctuation. Encourage them to write their thoughts quickly and freely.

Revise and create a final draft. Remind students to use the Revising and Editing Checklist (Master 11) to guide them in revising their writing. Have students review each other's writing and give each other feedback on the parts of the letter that are logical, clear, and interesting, and the parts that need revision.

When students have finished revising their writing, use the Writing Rubric (Master 10) to evaluate it. Be sure you review your response with each student so he or she understands the strengths and weaknesses of this piece of writing. Have students date the writing and put the completed pieces in their writing portfolios.

Building Fluency

Identify small sections from "Hola, Congresswoman." Tell students that they will use paired reading to read these sections aloud. Put students into groups of two. Give them time to read a passage silently 2–3 times to encourage their best oral reading. Partners take turns being the reader or listener. After the first reading, the listener does not provide feedback. After the second and third readings, the listener provides feedback to the reader. Remind students to pay attention to words that cause them to stumble and to read for the author's message. Their goal is to read the passage as fluently as if they were just speaking.

Everyone's a Winner

Lesson Overview: (PAGE 65)

Theme

Have students read the lesson title on page 65 and tell them that the title introduces the lesson theme, Sports and Recreation. Discuss the theme by having students make personal connections, sharing their favorite sport to watch or play. Ask students what types of recreation facilities are available in their communities.

Learning Objectives

Be sure students understand the outcome of each of the learning goals.

- *Read a story about two brothers and their favorite sports.* Point out that this story is fiction. It has characters who are not real, but their story is like the stories of people whom we all know.
- *Learn to compare and contrast ideas.*
- *Master the key vocabulary used in the story.*
- *Write a recommendation.*

Preteach the vocabulary. (PAGE 65)

Read the key vocabulary words and their definitions to the students. Tell them that they will recognize all these words in the story.

- Distribute the Vocabulary Knowledge Rating Chart (Master 9) and have students individually rate each of the key vocabulary words.
- Review particularly challenging words with students by listing each one on the board, modeling its use in a sentence, and having two or three students use the word in original sentences. Reframe student sentences that do not use the new words correctly.

You may wish to offer a mini-lesson on adjectives as students read the respective parts of speech with the definitions of the vocabulary words. [See page 41 in this book for a mini-lesson on adjectives. Use Master 5 or 6 to give students practice in recognizing adjectives.]

Before You Read (PAGE 66)

Explain to students that when they read fiction, it is important to stay focused on the plot of the story. This may involve summarizing the plot as they are reading. Suggest that they develop the habit of reading with a pencil or highlighter and sticky notes or a small notebook available. When reading a story, students might use a highlighter to mark important events in the plot and sticky notes to jot down questions or predictions they have as they read.

As students begin to write answers to the questions for each element on page 66, have them read the respective Think About Its.

Use what you know. Use the Think About It to elicit discussion about students' favorite sports to watch and to play. In answering questions, students may indicate that they prefer playing one sport and watching another. Have students share how they prefer to watch sporting events: going to live events or watching sports on television. Have them give reasons for their preferences.

Preview the story. Have students discuss how the title "Score!" suggests that the story is probably related to sports. Ask students to predict from the illustration on page 67 the sports the title is referring to.

Reading the Story (PAGES 67–69)

Emphasize to students that reading to find out why the two brothers disagree gives them a purpose for reading the story. It is a question to answer as they read. Highlighting phrases that also indicate how the two sports differ will keep students involved with the text.

Side-Column Vocabulary Remind students that the vocabulary words and phrases in the side column have been selected as important to the theme and content of the story. These words may be useful in the context of sports and recreation, but they are not necessarily part of everyday language.

Mid-Passage Questions The answers to the questions call on students' judgments, so there are no right or wrong answers. Review students' written answers to assess whether they are getting meaning from the text. They should be able to support each of their answers with evidence from the story.

After You Read (PAGES 70–71)

Build a robust vocabulary. Ask students to check their answers in the answer keys in their books.

Think about your reading. Ask students to check their answers in the answer keys in their books. Ask additional questions to enrich the discussion so that students will be better able to write about sports. Here are some possible questions:

- As you were reading, what did the author want you to think Angelo was drawing on his notepad? What was Angelo actually drawing? Why did this make the brothers laugh? (page 69)

- The brothers took their nephew to a basketball game and a baseball game so that he could decide which sport he preferred. What else could they have done to help their nephew choose a favorite sport?

Extend the reading. Here are some additional activities to expand students' understanding:

- Students may enjoy taking parts and reading the dialogues aloud. Most of the text of "Score!" is written as dialogue, so invite pairs or trios of students to choose a section to practice and then read for the class. Encourage students to read with as much natural expression as they can.

- *For English Language Learners* Sentence combining is particularly helpful when comparing and contrasting, so that sentences are less choppy. Make two columns on the board. Under Column A, have students dictate short sentences describing baseball, for example: *Most professional games are played outside.*

Under Column B, have students dictate short sentences describing basketball, for example: *Most professional games are played inside.* Model for students how to combine sentences using *and* or *but*: *Most professional baseball games are played outside, but most professional basketball games are played inside.* Encourage volunteers to combine a sentence from Column A with a sentence from Column B, using *but* for contrasting and *and* for comparing.

- Work with students to generate a list of topics to compare and contrast. High-interest ideas might include two sports, restaurants, political figures, or movies. Have pairs or small groups of students create Venn Diagrams in which they compare and contrast the two things or ideas. Invite groups to share their Venn Diagrams with the class, being sure to present each idea in a complete sentence.

- At home, have each student create a simple pamphlet or flier promoting his or her favorite sport. Students should include a brief description of the rules of the sport and perhaps a drawing or illustration. Invite students to present their pamphlets in small groups in class.

Use reading skills: Compare and contrast. Explain to students that comparing and contrasting shows how two things or ideas are the same or different. After reading the story, readers can compare and contrast basketball and baseball. By looking at similar elements of each sport, it is possible to discuss what is the same and what is different about the two sports. Students will enjoy commenting on the levels of intensity, the complexity of the rules, the role of the coach, and how much strategy is involved in each game.

Use a graphic organizer. In this lesson the Venn Diagram gives students the opportunity to analyze how two things or ideas are the same and different. A Venn Diagram also helps the reader or writer ensure that he or she is comparing the two things or ideas along similar dimensions. The diagram highlights the visual relationship between the ideas in the text.

Write About It (PAGES 73–74)

Write a recommendation. Have students read the directions on page 73. Be sure they understand that they will write their opinion about the best sport for the community center to sponsor.

Prewriting Students will use the graphic organizer to compare and contrast basketball and baseball. Encourage students to compare the sports along the same dimensions. After organizing the facts, they should decide which sport to recommend. They can use the contrasts in their diagrams to support their recommendations.

Thinking Beyond Reading Have students work with a partner or a small group to discuss the questions. The intent is for students to probe more deeply and to elaborate on the topic by addressing issues around recommending a sport that did not arise when they were first brainstorming. Encourage them to add ideas to their graphic organizers.

Write a draft. Have students write independently. Write on the board the following sample topic sentence: *I think _____ would be the better sport for the community center to choose.* Be sure students understand that all the sentences in the paragraph must relate to the same main idea. Remind students to use the ideas in their graphic organizers to organize the different elements of their responses. These will be the details in their paragraphs. While drafting, students should not be concerned with spelling or punctuation. Encourage them to write their thoughts quickly and freely.

Revise and create a final draft. Remind students to use the Revising and Editing Checklist (Master 11) to guide them in revising their writing. Have students review each other's writing and give each other feedback on the parts of the paragraph that are logical, clear, and interesting, and the parts that need revision.

When students have finished revising their writing, use the Writing Rubric (Master 11) to evaluate it. Be sure you review your response with each student so he or she understands the strengths and weaknesses of this piece of writing. Have students date the writing and put the completed pieces in their writing portfolios.

Building Fluency

Identify small sections from "Score!" Tell students that they will use paired reading to read these sections aloud. Put students into groups of two. Give them time to read a passage silently 2–3 times to encourage their best oral reading. Partners take turns being the reader or listener. After the first reading, the listener does not provide feedback. After the second and third readings, the listener provides feedback to the reader. Remind students to pay attention to words that cause them to stumble and to read for the author's message. Their goal is to read the passage as fluently as if they were just speaking.

The Way It Was

Lesson Overview: (PAGE 75)

Theme

Have students read the lesson title on page 75, and tell them that the title introduces the lesson theme, Housing and Transportation. Discuss the theme by having students make personal connections, telling what type of transportation they prefer to use for traveling long distances. Ask students if they have ever ridden on a train, either in the United States or overseas.

Learning Objectives

Be sure students understand the outcome of each of the learning goals.

- *Learn about the Pullman porters of the 1920s.* Point out that this article is nonfiction. It gives factual information about a group of African American workers who made history in the early 20th century.
- *Learn to make inferences.*
- *Master the key vocabulary used in the article.*
- *Write a summary.*

Preteach the vocabulary. (PAGE 75)

Read the key vocabulary words and their definitions to the students. Tell them that they will recognize all these words in the article.

- Distribute the Vocabulary Knowledge Rating Chart (Master 9) and have students individually rate each of the key vocabulary words.
- Review particularly challenging words with students by listing each one on the board, modeling its use in a sentence, and having two or three students use the word in original sentences. Reframe student sentences that do not use the new words correctly.

You may wish to offer a mini-lesson on verbs as students read the respective parts of speech with the definitions of the vocabulary words. [See page 40 of this book for a mini-lesson on verbs. Use Master 3 or 4 to give students practice in recognizing verbs.]

Before You Read (PAGE 76)

Explain to students that good readers get involved with what they read. One of the strategies they use to increase their involvement is to ask and answer questions about the text as they read. Suggest that they use sticky notes to write down their questions and a highlighter to mark phrases that answer those questions. An alternative strategy is to put question marks in the margin where they find ideas they do not understand. After marking a confusing passage, a good reader forms questions and then rereads to find the answers.

As students begin to write answers to the questions for each element on page 76, have them read the respective Think About Its.

Use what you know.   Use the Think About It to elicit discussion about the issues students have had when looking for good jobs. They may wish to discuss other work-related problems they or others they know have dealt with.

Ask yourself questions.   Have students read the title and the first section of "The Pullman Porters" and write three questions that come to their minds as they read that passage. Have students write those questions on sticky notes and use a highlighter as they read to highlight phrases that offer answers to the questions. Discuss their questions and answers.

Reading the Story (PAGES 77–79)

Emphasize to students that they will read about the good and bad aspects of being a Pullman porter. This will give them a purpose for reading the passage. To keep them involved in the article, suggest that students underline sentences that refer to the pros and cons of the job.

Side-Column Vocabulary Remind students that the vocabulary words and phrases in the side column have been selected as important to the theme and content of the article. These words may be useful in the context of trains and work, but they are not necessarily part of everyday language.

Mid-Passage Questions Some of the answers to the questions call on students' judgments, so there are not many right or wrong answers. Review students' written answers to assess whether they are getting meaning from the text. They should indicate in their answers that some African American men felt the job of porter was acceptable because the pay was good and the work was steady. Ask students to share their feelings about the job. Would they have been willing to do it?

After You Read (PAGES 80–82)

Build a robust vocabulary. Ask students to check their answers in the answer keys in their books.

Think about your reading. Ask students to check their answers in the answer keys in their books. Ask additional questions to enrich the discussion so that students will be better able to write their summaries later. Here are some possible questions:

- Apply what you have read to picture the inside of a Pullman car and how it affects the porters' work. How many seats are there? How many beds? Are there windows? What else do you visualize?

- The author states that the Pullman Company went out of business because "People took cars or planes instead." Why do you think people chose cars or planes over trains? If you were traveling a long distance, would you choose to travel by plane, car, or train? Why?

Extend the reading. Here are some additional activities to expand students' understanding.

- Students may enjoy dramatizing some parts of the article, such as preparing a sleeper car, ensuring that the passengers are not sick, or negotiating for better working conditions. Ask

students to write a script for the part they will dramatize.

- *For English Language Learners* Encourage students to look through the text of the article and circle verbs that are in the past tense. Have students write the past tense verbs on sticky notes and then organize them according to the spelling rules they follow (add -ed, double the consonant and add -ed, change the y to i and add -ed, no rule.) Have students write original sentences using a variety of past-tense verbs from the article.

- At home, have each student compare and contrast his or her last long trip with a fictional trip on a Pullman train. Encourage students to compare the trips in terms of comfort, speed, view, and flexibility, among other things. Have students share their work in small groups during the next class meeting.

Use reading skills: Make inferences. Explain to students that authors do not always state everything they wish to convey. Sometimes, authors imply, or suggest, things and leave it to the reader to infer what is meant. In "The Pullman Porters," the author does not always state the porters' feelings about their situations. The readers must "read between the lines" and use the information in the text combined with how they would feel if they had been porters to infer how the porters and other African Americans felt. Tell students that making these types of inferences may require what is often described as "putting themselves in another's shoes."

Use a graphic organizer. The inference chart in this lesson shows students that they must support the inferences they are making with information from the text. It shows how the ideas in the text and what the reader believes is true can lead to an inference.

Write About It (PAGES 83–84)

Write a summary. Have students read the directions on page 83 and be sure they understand that they will write a summary of one particular section of the article.

Prewriting Remind students that summaries give only the main points. They will find the main points of "The Good News" section of the article, which are all advantages of being a Pullman porter, and put them in the graphic organizer. Then they will use this information to write the summary.

Thinking Beyond Reading Have students work with a partner or a small group to discuss the questions. The intent is for students to probe more deeply and to make sure they include the most important advantages of being a Pullman porter. Remind them that their summaries should include all of the major points and none of the unimportant details.

Write a draft. Have students write independently. Write on the board the following topic sentence: *There were advantages to being a Pullman porter.* Be sure that students understand that all the sentences in the paragraph must relate to this main idea. Remind students to use the ideas in their charts to give specific examples to support the topic sentence. These will be the details in their paragraphs. While drafting, students should not be concerned with spelling or punctuation. Encourage them to write their thoughts quickly and freely.

Revise and create a final draft. Remind students to use the Revising and Editing Checklist (Master 11) to guide them in revising their writing. Have students review each other's writing and give each other feedback on the parts of the paragraph that are logical, clear, and interesting, and the parts that need revision.

When students have finished revising their writing, use the Writing Rubric (Master 10) to evaluate it. Be sure you review your response with each student so he or she understands the strengths and weaknesses of this piece of writing. Have students date the writing and put the completed pieces in their writing portfolios.

Building Fluency

Identify small sections from "The Pullman Porters." Tell students that they will use paired reading to read these sections aloud. Put students into groups of two. Give them time to read a passage silently 2–3 times to encourage their best oral reading. Partners take turns being the reader or listener. After the first reading, the listener does not provide feedback. After the second and third readings, the listener provides feedback to the reader. Remind students to pay attention to words that cause them to stumble and to read for the author's message. Their goal is to read the passage as fluently as if they were just speaking.

Food Around the World

Lesson Overview: (PAGE 85)

Theme

Have students read the lesson title on page 85 and tell them that the title introduces the lesson theme, Food. Discuss the theme by having students make personal connections, naming their favorite foods and describing a typical dinner for their family. Have students share memories of meals they shared with someone from a different culture. How was the meal different from what they are used to?

Learning Objectives

Be sure students understand the outcome of each of the learning goals.

- *Learn about foods in different countries.* Explain that this article is nonfiction. It gives accurate information about different foods eaten by people around the world.
- *Learn to synthesize information.*
- *Master the key vocabulary words used in the article.*
- *Write a paragraph about a personal experience.*

Preteach the vocabulary. (PAGE 85)

Read the key vocabulary words and their definitions to the students. Tell them that they will recognize all these words in the article.

- Distribute the Vocabulary Knowledge Rating Chart (Master 9) and have students individually rate each of the key vocabulary words.
- Review particularly challenging words with students by listing each one on the board, modeling its use in a sentence, and having two or three students use the word in original sentences. Reframe student sentences that do not use the new words correctly.

You may wish to offer a mini-lesson on adjectives as students read the respective parts of speech with the definitions of the vocabulary words. [See page 41 of this book for a mini-lesson on adjectives. Use Master 5 or 6 to give students practice in recognizing adjectives.]

Before You Read (PAGE 86)

Explain that good readers seek the best strategies for interacting with a particular text. "What's for Dinner?" is a nonfiction text, so students will need to choose strategies that help them to organize and retain information, as well as strategies that help them to ask and answer questions about the information provided. Tell students that active readers go back after they complete the text to review what they have written.

As students begin to write answers to the questions for each element on page 86, have them read the respective Think About Its.

Use what you know. Use the Think About It to elicit discussion about students' practices and preferences around food and eating. Encourage students to talk about how their traditions are similar to or different from traditions of others in the class.

Make predictions while you read. Have students read the first two paragraphs of "What's for Dinner?" and then read the Think About It. Ask them to predict what they'll learn about in the article. Suggest that they check to see if their predictions are correct as they read. That is one way to be an active reader.

Reading the Article (PAGES 87–89)

Emphasize to students that they will read to find out about foods in at least three different countries. It is information for them to look for as they read. Recording the names of countries and dishes on sticky notes will keep students actively involved in the reading.

Side-Column Vocabulary Remind students that the vocabulary words and phrases in the side column have been selected as important to the theme and content of the story. These words may be useful in the context of foods in other countries, but they are not necessarily part of everyday language.

Mid-Passage Questions Some of the answers to the questions call on students' judgments, so there are not many right or wrong answers. Review students' written answers to assess whether they are getting meaning from the text. They should indicate in their answers how climate affects food choices, and they should support their answers with evidence from the text. Ask if anyone learned about a food they'd like to try.

After You Read (PAGES 90–93)

Build a robust vocabulary. Ask students to check their answers in the answer keys in their books.

Think about your reading. Ask students to check their answers in the answer keys in their books. Ask additional questions to enrich the discussion so that students will be better able to write about a visit to an interesting restaurant. Here are some possible questions:

- Describe a food that you like and how it is the same or different from one of the dishes described in the article. You might choose to compare and contrast the dish you like with borscht, beef stroganoff, fondue, or iguana. Talk about the ingredients in the dish, how it is prepared, and what it looks and tastes like.

- The author uses the words *weird* and *unusual* in describing certain foods. How do you think people's tastes for different foods develop? Do you think that people who eat iguana, snake, or dragonflies think those foods are unusual? Why or why not? Can you think of any foods that you like to eat that someone in another culture might describe as weird or unusual?

Extend the reading. Here are some additional activities to expand students' understanding:

- Students may enjoy pretending that they own unusual restaurants. Have students use

information from the text to create television commercials for their restaurants. For example, a student might choose to advertise an Indonesian dragonfly restaurant. The student would share information from the *Weird or Wonderful* section, and entice readers to look forward to eating deep-fried dragonflies. You may wish to model this activity.

- *For English Language Learners* Remind students that commas serve many purposes in English. One of those purposes is to separate three or more words in a series. Have students find examples of series of things in the text (*China, Hong Kong, Thailand, and Korea; carrots, onions, and celery; borscht, pelmini, or stroganoff*) and then determine the rule (commas between each thing and before the *and* or *or*.) Invite pairs of students to write original sentences which include series separated by commas.

- Encourage students to describe a person they are fond of. Have students share four characteristics about that person. Invite a volunteer to synthesize those details into a summary statement. You may wish to model this activity for students: My *father works hard as a storekeeper. He keeps his accounts organized and his stock fresh and attractive. Everyone in the neighborhood shops at his store. People shop at his store rather than the Supermart down the street.* A summary statement: My *father is a good, well-respected businessman.*

- Have each student interview somebody born in a different culture. Have the student ask about the most unusual food that person has eaten: *What was it? How was it prepared? What did it look and taste like? Would they eat it again?* Have students share what they have learned.

Use reading skills: Synthesize information. Explain to students that texts are often written so that the main idea is clearly stated and supporting details are provided to back up that main idea. Sometimes, however, the supporting details are provided and the reader is expected to synthesize those details into a main idea. Remind students that they read in the article about foods eaten in

Russian, Switzerland, Hong Kong, Mexico, and Bali. What did they learn about American eating habits by reading about the unusual foods? This can become a synthesizing statement.

Use a graphic organizer. In this lesson the table gives the reader a structure for listing and keeping track of the important ideas from the text. These ideas can be synthesized into a final statement. This type of graphic organizer helps prevent the reader from getting lost in the details.

Write About It (PAGES 93–94)

Write a paragraph about a personal experience. Have students read the directions on page 93. Be sure they understand that they will write a paragraph about an experience at a restaurant.

Prewriting In developing their ideas for the graphic organizer, students will consider all of the events and details that occurred at the restaurant. They may wish to write their ideas on sticky notes first. This allows them to reorder the events.

Thinking Beyond Reading Have students work with a partner or a small group to discuss the questions. The intent is for students to probe more deeply and to elaborate on the topic by addressing issues that did not arise when they were first thinking about their restaurant visits. Encourage them to add ideas to their graphic organizers.

Write a draft. Have students write independently. Write on the board the following topic sentence: *I had a meal at an interesting restaurant recently.* Be sure that students

understand that all the sentences in the paragraph must relate to the same main idea, in this case their trip to a restaurant. Remind students to use the ideas in their graphic organizers to develop their responses. Encourage them to synthesize the details with a summary statement. While drafting, students should not be concerned with spelling or punctuation. Encourage them to write their thoughts quickly and freely.

Revise and create a final draft. Remind students to use the Revising and Editing Checklist (Master 11) to guide them in revising their writing. Have students review each other's writing and give each other feedback on the parts of the paragraph that are logical, clear, and interesting, and the parts that need revision.

When students have finished revising their writing, use the Writing Rubric (Master 10) to evaluate it. Be sure you review your response with each student so he or she understands the strengths and weaknesses of this piece of writing. Have students date the writing and put the completed pieces in their writing portfolios.

Building Fluency

Identify small sections from "What's for Dinner?" Tell students that they will use echo reading to read these sections aloud. Put students into groups of two. Give them time to read a passage silently 2–3 times to encourage their best oral reading. Remind them to pay attention to words that cause them to stumble. They will imitate your phrasing and intonation for each sentence. Remind students to use punctuation and typographic cues to add expression to their reading. Tell them that the goal is to read the passage as fluently as if they were just speaking.

Buying and Selling

Lesson Overview: (PAGE 95)

Theme

Have students read the lesson title on page 95 and tell them that the title introduces the lesson theme, Consumerism and Money. Discuss the theme by having students make personal connections, telling if they have ever had anything stolen from them. Ask students if they have ever seen someone selling stolen goods. What did the scene look like? How did they know the goods were stolen?

Learning Objectives

Be sure students understand the outcome of each of the learning goals.

- *Read a story about teens who buy and sell stolen goods.* Point out that this story is fiction, but the situation it deals with happens in real life and the characters in the story are like people they might know.
- *Learn to draw conclusions.*
- *Master the key vocabulary used in the story.*
- *Write a journal entry.*

Preteach the vocabulary. (PAGE 95)

Read the key vocabulary words and their definitions to the students. Tell them that they will recognize all these words in the story.

- Distribute the Vocabulary Knowledge Rating Chart (Master 9) and have students individually rate each of the key vocabulary words.
- Review particularly challenging words with students by listing each one on the board, modeling its use in a sentence, and having two or three students use the word in original sentences. Reframe student sentences that do not use the new words correctly.

You may wish to offer a mini-lesson on adverbs as students read the respective parts of speech with the definitions of the vocabulary words. [See page 42 of this book for a mini-lesson on adverbs. Use Master 7 or 8 to give students practice in recognizing adverbs.]

Before You Read (PAGE 96)

Explain that good readers connect with the text and remain engaged as they read. Active readers also write and highlight as they are reading, and they return to those notes in order to check their understanding. Point out that when reading fiction, it is important to pause occasionally and summarize the plot. Suggest to students that they develop the habit of reading with a pencil and sticky notes or a small notebook available. Using these tools will help them stay engaged with the text.

As students begin to write answers to the questions for each element on page 96, have them read the respective Think About Its.

Ask yourself questions. Have students discuss how the title, "The Devil's Deal," suggests that something evil or dark will happen. The picture on page 97 may suggest questions students have about it and the story. Explore these in a discussion.

Visualize the action in the story. Explain that good readers visualize the characters and the action in a story to enhance their understanding. Students may picture themselves as one of the teens gathered around Sam at the beginning of the story. After students have read the first section of the story, have them read the Think About It. What did they see and hear? What would they feel if they were part of that scene? Can they imagine themselves in Max's shoes?

Reading the Story (PAGES 97–99)

Emphasize to students that they will read to find out how far Max will go to get what he wants. It is a question to answer as they read. To keep them involved in the story, suggest that students keep track of the steps Max goes through to get his Sajo, numbering them in the margin.

Side-Column Vocabulary Remind students that the vocabulary words and phrases in the side column have been selected as important to the theme and content of the story. These words may be useful in the context of crime and theft, but they are not necessarily part of everyday language.

Mid-Passage Questions Some of the answers to the questions call on students' judgments, so there are not many right or wrong answers. Review students' written answers to assess whether they are getting meaning from the text. They should indicate in their answers that the Sajo is an interesting and expensive new electronic device. Students should support their answers with evidence from the text or from their own experience. Ask students if they agree with Max's reasoning about how to acquire a Sajo.

After You Read (PAGES 100–102)

Build a robust vocabulary. Ask students to check their answers in the answer keys in their books.

Think about your reading. Ask students to check their answers in the answer keys in their books. Ask additional questions to enrich the discussion so that students will be better able to write about buying stolen goods. Here are some possible questions:

- A good reader reads to discover how the characters are feeling. Sometimes the author will describe a character's tone and body language rather than tell the reader explicitly how the character feels. "Sam looked around quickly, frowning. When he saw they were alone, he shook his head. . . , his voice low and quiet." What was Sam thinking and feeling during this exchange with Max? What other examples of tone and body language can you find in the text that give you clues to what a character is thinking and feeling?

- When Max went to George's apartment, the author writes, "For a second, Max hesitated." Why do you think Max hesitated? At what additional points in the story might Max have been able to change his mind about buying the stolen Sajo?

Extend the reading. Here are some additional activities to expand students' understanding:

- Students may enjoy taking parts and reading the dialogues aloud. Max's conversations with Sam or George offer good opportunities for students to practice reading aloud. Have a narrator read the non-dialogue parts. Encourage students to read with as much natural expression as they can.

- *For English Language Learners* Tell students to look in the first part of the story for the following phrases and expressions that don't mean exactly what the words say: *at lightning speed, sweet, learn a lesson*. Have students read the expressions in the context of the sentences and explain what they think the phrases mean. Model for them additional sentences that use the phrases correctly until students understand their proper usage in English. Have students try to use these phrases in original sentences. Reframe the sentences that do not use the phrases correctly. Remind students to add these phrases to their personal dictionaries.

- Outside of class, have students poll and record people's responses to the following question: *Would you ever consider buying something you really needed or wanted knowing that it might have been stolen?* Have students write paragraphs summarizing the results of their surveys and drawing conclusions about people's feelings about purchasing stolen goods.

Use reading skills: Draw conclusions. Explain to students that experienced readers are able to combine what the text says with what they already know about people's behavior in order to draw conclusions about characters and their motivations.

Use a graphic organizer. In this lesson the chart visually organizes for the reader what he or she has read in the text, the ideas the reader brings from his or her life experiences, and the conclusions that come from putting these things together.

Write About It (PAGES 103–104)

Write a journal entry. Remind students that their journal entries should be brief and to the point in their analyses of the problem and the conclusions they will come to. Be sure they understand that they will analyze both sides of the argument in order to come to their conclusions.

Prewriting Remind students that although they may have strong opinions one way or another on this issue, there are arguments on both sides. Encourage students to fill in their graphic organizers as completely as possible, including as many ideas as they can think of on both sides of the issue.

Thinking Beyond Reading Have students work with a partner or a small group to discuss the questions. The intent is for students to probe more deeply and to elaborate on the topic by addressing issues that did not arise when they were first thinking about buying stolen goods. Since different people have different views and opinions on the matter, a discussion of this topic should lead to many additional ideas for students' writing. Encourage them to add ideas to their graphic organizers.

Write a draft. Have students write independently. Tell students that journals are written from the first person point of view. Remind students to use the ideas in their graphic organizers to organize their responses. These will be the details in their paragraphs. While drafting, students should not be concerned with spelling or punctuation. Encourage them to write their thoughts quickly and freely.

Revise and create a final draft. Remind students to use the Revising and Editing Checklist (Master 11) to guide them in revising their writing. Have students review each other's writing and give each other feedback on the parts of the paragraph that are logical, clear, and interesting, and the parts that need revision.

When students have finished revising their writing, use the Writing Rubric (Master 10) to evaluate it. Be sure you review your response with each student so he or she understands the strengths and weaknesses of this piece of writing. Have students date the writing and put the completed pieces in their writing portfolios.

Building Fluency

Identify small sections from "The Devil's Deal." Tell students that they will use paired reading to read these sections aloud. Put students into groups of two. Give them time to read a passage silently 2–3 times to encourage their best oral reading. Partners take turns being the reader or listener. After the first reading, the listener does not provide feedback. After the second and third readings, the listener provides feedback to the reader. Remind students to pay attention to words that cause them to stumble and to read for the author's message. Their goal is to read the passage as fluently as if they were just speaking.

Grammar Mini-Lessons

LESSON 1: NOUNS

Learning Objectives

To define the term *noun*

To identify nouns

To generate nouns

Activate Prior Knowledge

Help students recall or find out what they know about *nouns*. Invite the class to play a guessing game. Ask a volunteer to think of an item that is made up of different parts. (Examples: *engine, dress, apartment*) Then have the volunteer name four parts, one at a time, while the class tries to name the thing. (Examples: *engine—carburetor, spark plugs, pistons, belts; dress—collar, sleeves, buttons, belt; apartment—windows, doors, kitchen, bedroom*) When the game is finished, tell the class that both the item and the parts are **nouns.**

Instruction

Tell the class that **nouns are the names of people, places, things, and ideas.** Write this definition on the board. Have students create a noun chart.

Examples of Nouns			
People	**Places**	**Things**	**Ideas**

To help them get started, ask students to think about places they have wanted to go to for a vacation. Have them take turns naming people, places, things, and ideas they would experience at each place. (Examples: *beach—swimmers, sunshine, surfboard, tranquility; city—museums, restaurants, shows, taxis, excitement*)

If students suggest proper nouns, include them, and point out that proper nouns are written with a capital letter at the beginning of each word.

If students seem to be having difficulty with nouns as "ideas," consider telling them the following: *The names of ideas are not things that you can touch with your hands. But they are still nouns, just like names of people, places, and things.* Examples might include the names of emotions such as *happiness* and *sadness* or American ideals such as *freedom* and *independence*.

Noun Practice

For more student practice with nouns, distribute Master 1 or 2 in this Teacher's Guide.

LESSON 2: VERBS

Learning Objectives
To define the term *verb*

To identify verbs

To generate verbs

Activate Prior Knowledge
Help students recall or discover what they already know about *verbs*. Ask a volunteer to go to the front of the class and, without moving his or her feet, move his or her body in as many different poses as possible. Tell the volunteer to hold each pose for enough time for the class to call out words to identify the action. (Examples: *bend, twist, bow, kneel, reach, flex, crouch*) Point out that each word they used to identify an action is a **verb.**

Instruction
Tell students that **verbs are words that show action.** Look at a volunteer and firmly say, "Stand!" and then "Sit!" Using the same body language and tone of voice, quickly say to another student, "Yellow!" and then "Four!" Tell the class you are making the point that words such as *yellow* and *four* do not name an action. Words such as *stand* and *sit* do. They are **verbs.**

Write the following two words on the board: *cries, baby*. Ask students to identify the word that shows action (*cries*). Continue to provide word pairs, giving each student an opportunity to decide which word is the verb. (Examples: *screech/monkey, chalk/write, rhyme/poet, purr/cat, sweep/broom*)

On the board, write a few common verbs, such as *sleep, sing,* and *walk*. Then ask students to list other similar verbs. If it would help, write "I _____ in the afternoon" on the board and ask students to complete the sentence. Encourage them to think of colorful verbs. (Examples: I *sleep/snooze/doze/nap/crash/drop/collapse* in the afternoon. He *sings/croons/hums/serenades/warbles/belts/raps* in the afternoon. They *walk/stroll//trample/wander/trudge/plod/ hike* in the afternoon.)

You may wish to encourage students to complete the following sentences with verbs: *Yesterday I _____. Today I _____. Tomorrow I _____.* Point out that the verbs they use show time.

Verb Practice
For more student practice with verbs, distribute Master 3 or 4 in this Teacher's Guide.

LESSON 3: ADJECTIVES

Learning Objectives
To define the term *adjective*

To identify adjectives

To generate adjectives

Activate Prior Knowledge
Help students recall or find out what they already know about *adjectives*. Ask a volunteer to name his or her favorite color. Write the color on the board. Then ask volunteers to take turns describing that color. (Examples: *green—cool, bright, soothing, fresh; red—warm, hot, dangerous, exciting; black—dark, inky, quiet, gloomy*) Point out to students that the words they are using are **adjectives.**

Instruction
Tell the class that **adjectives are words that describe nouns.** They answer the questions *How many?* and *What kind?* Tell the class that you will illustrate the concept of adjectives by doing an inventory of classroom supplies. On the board draw a chart like the one below. Include a noun of your choice in the first box.

Noun	Adjectives	
	How many?	**What kind?**
pencils		

Tell the class you'd like to make sure you have all essential classroom items. Model the task by guiding students through the first item, asking volunteers to find out, for example, *How many pencils do we have?* Write the number in the appropriate column. (Example: *28*) Then ask *What kind of pencils?* and fill in their responses. (Examples: *black, number 2*) Point out that the answers to the questions *How many?* and *What kind?* are **adjectives,** or words that describe nouns.

After you've modeled the first item, ask for names of more items from volunteers.

You may wish to point out to students that nouns often are described by more than one adjective. As an example, write a sentence on the board that uses both a noun and its adjectives from the chart. (Example: *There are 28 black pencils in the storage cabinet.*) Point out that both *28* and *black* are adjectives that describe the noun *pencils*. Also, *storage* describes *cabinet.*

Suggest to students that they conduct their own personal inventories, using nouns and adjectives. The inventories can be of kitchen pantry items, clothing in the bedroom closet, or a child's toys or books. Ask students to write several sentences using the nouns and adjectives from their inventories. Encourage them to use more than one adjective to describe each noun.

Adjective Practice
For more student practice with adjectives, distribute Master 5 or 6 in this Teacher's Guide.

LESSON 4: ADVERBS

Learning Objectives
To define the term *adverb*

To identify adverbs

To generate adverbs

Activate Prior Knowledge
Help students recall or find out what they know about *adverbs*. Start a how-to discussion. Tell students about a recent project of yours. (Examples: built a shelf, painted a portrait, or wrote a story about children on a playground) Ask the class to describe briefly what steps were involved in such a project. Write on the board the verb and adverbs they use. (Examples: *hammered loudly, measured carefully*) Underline the adverbs. Tell the class that adverbs describe how, when, and where an action (the verb) occurred.

Instruction
Tell the class that **adverbs are words that describe verbs.** They tell how, when, or where. Draw the following chart on the board.

Verb	How?	When?	Where?
write	quietly	yesterday	outside

Tell the class that you would like them to help you fill in the chart. Model the process. Tell the class you are thinking about your project (writing a story about children on a playground). Write the verb *write* in the first column. And then *quietly, yesterday,* and *outside* in the remaining columns. Then ask the class, "I did what?" Elicit that you wrote a story quietly outside yesterday.

Ask volunteers for other action verbs. Write one in the first column. Help students through the process again twice, using adverbs that describe the verbs they provide.

(Examples: *Steal—How does he steal second base? Slyly, quickly; When does he steal second base? Often, sometimes; Where does he steal first base? Outside, there;* More examples: *snore, loudly/often/everywhere; flies, gracefully/usually/overhead; moves, cautiously/always/backward; runs, quickly/today/indoors*)

Point out to students that adverbs may appear anywhere in a sentence. Often they are close to the verb, but sometimes they are not. Write examples on the board. Draw an arrow from the adverb to the verb. Examples:

The driver honked the horn <u>loudly</u>.

<u>Loudly</u>, the driver honked the horn.

The driver <u>loudly</u> honked the horn.

Adverb Practice
For more student practice with adverbs, distribute Master 7 or 8 in this Teacher's Guide.

Master 1: Nouns 1

Student's Name _____

> **A noun is the name of a person, place, thing, or idea.**

Examples of nouns are listed in the chart below.

People	Places	Things	Ideas
coach	studio	costume	fame
players	Chicago	spotlight	joy

Finding Nouns: Underline all the nouns in each sentence.

1. Muesli is a cereal made from a mixture of grains.

2. Wheat, oats, millet, and rice are usually in the box.

3. Boil the mixture slowly with milk or water in a pot.

4. Recipes may include sugar, cinnamon, or fruit.

5. Grits is a type of hot cereal made from corn.

6. A mill grinds the kernels into tiny bits.

7. Eat it for breakfast, lunch, dinner, or a snack.

8. Serve it with a little butter or try it with cheese.

Writing Nouns: The nouns in the box below are the names of ideas. Write one noun in each sentence.

health	faith	pride	distance	habit	progress

9. She went to the gym to improve her _____.

10. At first she made no _____ at all.

11. She could walk only a short _____.

12. But she refused to lose _____ in herself.

13. Exercise is now a daily _____.

14. You can see the _____ in her eyes.

Using Nouns: Write a noun to complete each sentence.

15. My favorite TV star is _____.

16. I usually eat _____ as a snack.

17. After I work out, I drink _____.

18. I go to the _____ whenever I can.

Master 2: Nouns 2

Student's Name _____

A noun is the name of a person, place, thing, or idea.

Common nouns are the general names for people, places, things, or ideas.
Proper nouns are the names of very specific people, places, or things.

	Common Nouns	**Proper Nouns**
People	woman	Tina Turner
Places	state	Tennessee
Things	song	"Proud Mary"

Finding Nouns: Underline the proper nouns. HINT: There may be more than one.

1. The city of New Orleans is where she lives.

2 Kathy Wilkerson is the first female firefighter there.

3. A woman named Molly was the first in New York City.

4. The Hudson River flows near the family home.

5. The children ride a horse on the Boston Post Road.

6. Tony joined the army in September of last year.

Writing Nouns: Write the common nouns in each sentence.

7. The town of Ripley is several miles away. _____

8. Anna Mae was born in the month of November. _____

9. She has a powerful voice and a unique style. _____

10. The woman often reads books about Buddha. _____

11. A boy listens to Miles Davis on the radio. _____

12. The saxophone is the horn Charlie plays. _____

13. Tina makes her home in Germany now. _____

Using Nouns: Write a proper noun for each common noun.

14. holiday _____

15. school _____

16. weekday _____

17. automobile _____

18. country _____

Master 3: Verbs 1

Student's Name _____

A verb is a word that shows action.

The underlined words are verbs. They show action.

Cities <u>hum</u>.　　Sabers <u>rattle</u>.　　Jets <u>soar</u>.
Trains <u>whistle</u>.　Flowers <u>bloom</u>.　Flags <u>wave</u>.

Finding Verbs: Circle the verb in each sentence. HINT: One sentence has two verbs.

1. Chad adopted a new name in Japan.

2. People call him "new dawn" or Akebono.

3. He grabs the man and thrusts him out of the ring.

4. The large athlete astonishes his fans.

5. He broke records year after year.

6. The wrestler suffered few losses in the ring.

7. He retired after a long, successful career.

Writing Verbs: Write the verb in each sentence.

8. Aquariums fascinate me. _____

9. We keep goldfish in our freshwater tank. _____

10. Most household fish live only six to eight years. _____

11. One rare type weighs as much as nine pounds. _____

12. People raised golden carp long ago in China. _____

13. An empress ordered a special pond for them. _____

14. Now I stare at my little fish for hours. _____

Using Verbs: For each verb, write another verb with the opposite meaning.

Example: laugh ____*cry*_____

15. win _____

16. give _____

17. start _____

18. smile _____

19. argue _____

20. whisper _____

21. lead _____

22. melt _____

23. fill _____

24. read _____

Master 4: Verbs 2

Student's Name _____

> **A verb is a word that shows action.**

The underlined words are verbs.

Verbs	**Time of Action**
The student <u>practices</u> for class.	present
She <u>worked</u> with a partner.	past
They <u>will succeed</u> together.	future

Finding Verbs: The verb in each sentence is underlined. Circle the time it shows.

1. He <u>was born</u> in Naples, Italy, in 1873.   future   past

2. The man <u>sounds</u> like an angel in heaven.   present   future

3. He <u>lived</u> a short but happy life.   past   present

4. He <u>sings</u> freely and with power.   future   present

5. We <u>will listen</u> to the tenor's voice later.   past   future

6. His high notes <u>will delight</u> you.   future   present

Writing Verbs: Write the verb in each sentence.

7. Julio plays chess around the world. _____

8. He earned the title of world champion. _____

9. Bobby received a lot of attention in his day. _____

10. The boy competes with adults in his class. _____

11. People will talk about the game on the Internet. _____

12. She will organize chess games for beginners. _____

Using Verbs: Underline the verbs. Then write each verb to show a different time.

Example: The child <u>waited</u> for her turn. ___*will wait*___

13. The red piece moves first. _____

14. The black one jumped the red. _____

15. The player captured the king. _____

16. The girl selects another checker. _____

17. It will force me into a corner. _____

46   Level 6 Master 4

Master 5: Adjectives 1

Student's Name _____

> ## An adjective is a word that describes a noun.

The adjectives in the sentences below are underlined.

Two hunters walk the trail.
The icy air pinches their cheeks.
The day ends with an orange sunset.

Finding Adjectives: The nouns are underlined in each sentence. Circle the adjective that describes each noun. HINT: There are nine adjectives.

1. Georgia was one of the first states in the union.

2. Atlanta is the largest city in this southern state.

3. A major product is its sweet peaches.

4. They have delicate flesh and an oval seed.

5. The juicy fruit ripens in late summer.

Writing Adjectives: Write the adjective that describes the underlined noun in each sentence.

6. The natives call it the great river. _____

7. Its fresh water flows into the gulf. _____

8. Catfish swim in the muddy depths. _____

9. A wailing hound picked up a scent. _____

10. It chases an exhausted fox down a hill. _____

11. The dog would not catch the lucky beast. _____

Using Adjectives: Complete each sentence. Write an adjective to describe each noun.

12. Climb up the _____ hills.

13. Dive into the _____ lakes.

14. Hike on the _____ trails.

15. Camp in the _____ tent.

16. Picnic by the _____ waterfall.

Master 6: Adjectives 2

Student's Name _____

An adjective is a word that describes a noun.

The adjectives in the sentences below are underlined.

Two youngsters dance to reggae music.
Their bright skirts swing to the happy rhythm.
Delighted onlookers tap their tired feet.

Finding Adjectives: Nouns are underlined in each sentence. Circle the adjectives that describe them.
HINT: There are 14 adjectives.

1. Green parks can be found in the busiest cities.

2. The urban forest offers a peaceful place for us to go.

3. One afternoon after a cool rain I went jogging.

4. A skinny youngster bikes along the busy path.

5. A frisky squirrel dives into a dark crevice of an old log.

6. Red cedars, western hemlocks, and leafy maples grow there.

Writing Adjectives: Complete each sentence by writing an adjective from the box.

pretty	brave	red	young	friendly	shy	yellow	old

7. The _____ woman bought the _____ dress.

8. The _____ policeman saved the _____ child.

9. The _____ man whistled for the _____ cab.

10. The _____ student looked at the _____ girl.

Using Adjectives: Write an adjective to complete each sentence.

11. They strolled down the _____ street.

12. They stopped at the _____ restaurant.

13. They sat at the _____ table.

14. They ordered the _____ salad.

15. They took the _____ bus back home.

Master 7: Adverbs 1

Student's Name _____

An adverb is a word that describes a verb.

These words are adverbs. They tell how, when, and where.

How?	kindly, slowly, loudly, timidly
When?	never, soon, today, sometimes
Where?	here, outside, nearby, nowhere

Finding Adverbs: Verbs are underlined in each sentence. Circle the adverbs that describe them.

1. Hugo regularly <u>attended</u> the public schools of Baltimore.

2. In sports, the young man's speed <u>served</u> him well.

3. He often <u>tutored</u> other high school students.

4. Some workers <u>complained</u> bitterly about low wages.

5. He later <u>became</u> an attorney in a city law firm.

6. The people wisely <u>elected</u> him mayor of the city.

7. A president gratefully <u>gave</u> him the Literacy Award.

Writing Adverbs: Write the adverb in each sentence. HINT: One sentence has two.

8. The new town swiftly grew to the size of a city. _____

9. Francis Scott Key famously wrote our anthem's lyrics there. _____

10. Our soldiers fought bravely in many wars. _____

11. At one time, the harbor had been nearly abandoned. _____

12. Now the Baltimore Orioles play ball at the park. _____

Using Adverbs: Rewrite each sentence using at least one adverb from the box.

outside	here	inside	rarely	always	today	again	there

13. He runs. _____

14. She sings. _____

15. He naps. _____

16. I raced. _____

17. He skips. _____

18. She snores. _____

19. I fell. _____

20. She grins. _____

Master 8: Adverbs 2

Student's Name _____

An adverb is a word that describes a verb.

The underlined words are adverbs. They describe verbs by telling how, when, and where.

She lives <u>happily</u>. (lives how?)

<u>Today</u> she sells soup. (sells when?)

The child plays <u>nearby</u>. (plays where?)

Finding Adverbs: The verbs are underlined. Circle each adverb that describes a verb.

1. They fearlessly <u>fought</u> for independence.

2. A doctor <u>treats</u> them there with herbs and medicines.

3. Remarkably, I <u>witnessed</u> some unusual weather.

4. People <u>talk</u> about these changes everywhere.

5. In my country, certain months <u>were</u> once cold and misty.

6. Now the growing season <u>is</u> over.

7. Rain usually <u>falls</u> throughout the year.

8. In summer, all the grasses <u>die</u> slowly.

9. Here in my village we <u>plan</u> for next year.

Writing Adverbs: Write the adverbs you circled in the correct column.

How?	When?	Where?
10.	13.	16.
11.	14.	17.
12.	15,	18.

Using Adverbs: Complete each sentence with an adverb from the box.

proudly	often	thoroughly	loudly	graciously

19. We heard about Kenyan food _____.

20. The host offers her hand _____.

21. She grinds the peanuts _____.

22. They _____ serve her tasty dish.

23. We slurp the soup _____.

Master 9: Vocabulary Knowledge Rating Chart   Student's Name

	1	2	3	4	5
Vocabulary Word	I know this word. I can explain its meaning and use it when I speak and write.	I think I know this word. It has something to do with _____.	I've seen or heard this word, but I'm not sure what it means.	I don't know this word. I need to learn it.	

Master 10: Writing Rubric

Student's Name

		Focus	Organization	Voice	Conventions
4		Ideas are on the topic and interesting.	There is a clearly presented main idea with supporting details, facts, and/or opinions. The writing flows very well.	The writer speaks to the audience clearly. Word choice is varied, and the words were chosen because they are the very best words for getting the point across.	Contains few, if any, errors in grammar, punctuation, capitalization, and/or spelling. Any errors that do occur do not get in the way of the reader's understanding.
3		Ideas are on the topic.	There is a main idea with supporting details, facts, and/or opinions. The writing flows.	The writer speaks to the audience. Word choice is varied and gets the point across.	Contains some errors in grammar, punctuation, capitalization, and/or spelling. These errors do not get in the way of the reader's understanding.
2		Ideas may be a bit off of the topic.	Although there is a main idea and/or details, the writing is sometimes difficult to follow.	The writer shows some understanding of the audience. Words are repeated too often and/or misused.	Contains several errors in grammar, punctuation, capitalization, and/or spelling. These errors may get in the way of the reader's understanding of the writing.
1		Ideas are not on the topic.	It is difficult for the reader to follow the writer's arguments or explanations.	The writer does not speak to the audience. Words are repeated too often and/or misused.	Contains serious errors in grammar, punctuation, capitalization, and/or spelling. These errors make the writing very difficult for the reader to understand.

Master 11: Revising and Editing Checklist   Student's Name

When you **revise,** you add to or take away from your writing to make it clearer and more understandable. It always helps to read your work to a partner so that you can make sure it is well organized, includes enough details, and makes sense.

When you **edit,** look at the specific words you have chosen. Are they the best words? Check your work for proper spelling, punctuation, and usage. Make sure that you have not left out or repeated words. Have you used correct grammar?

Always revise before you edit. You don't want to spend time editing something you may not include in your revision.

Revising

_____ I read the writing to myself to see if it made sense.

_____ I read the writing to a partner to see if it made sense.

_____ My writing stays on the topic.

_____ My paragraph has a topic sentence and includes supporting details.

_____ My writing is logical and well organized.

_____ The writing is interesting.

_____ I used enough information and examples to make my point.

_____ My ending ties up the writing.

Editing

_____ Each of my sentences ends with a period (.), a question mark (?), or an exclamation point (!).

_____ My subjects and verbs agree.

_____ I have used commas correctly.

_____ Each of my sentences begins with a capital letter.

_____ I have used quotation marks correctly.

_____ My paragraphs are indented.

_____ I chose my words carefully so that the reader can visualize just what I'm talking about.

_____ I inserted words that add interest to my writing.

_____ I inserted words that were missing.

_____ I deleted extra words that I didn't need.

_____ I circled words that I think may be incorrectly spelled. I used additional resources to check the spelling of those words.

_____ I gave my edited draft to a partner to check.

Master 12: Editor's Marks   Student's Name

Use these marks when editing a paper. Make sure you understand what the marks mean when a teacher or partner uses them on your paper.

Editing Marks		
≡	Changes a lowercase letter to an uppercase letter.	I visited kiwanis park with my cousins. ≡ ≡
/	Changes an uppercase letter to a lowercase letter.	Maria brought her Dog.
∧	Adds a word or punctuation mark.	We biked ∧ the park. *to*
ℓ	Deletes a word or punctuation mark.	We ran around the the playground.
☐	Indicates incorrect word choice.	We had a lot of fun their *there*
◯	Indicates a misspelled word.	We plan to go agin next weekend. *again*

Answers to Masters 1–8

MASTER 1: NOUNS 1
1. Muesli, cereal, mixture, grains
2. Wheat, oats, millet, rice, box
3. mixture, milk, water, pot
4. Recipes, sugar, cinnamon, fruit
5. Grits, type, cereal, corn
6. mill, kernels, bits
7. breakfast, lunch, dinner, snack
8. butter, cheese
9. health
10. progress
11. distance
12. faith
13. habit
14. pride
15.–18. Answers will vary.

MASTER 2: NOUNS 2
1. New Orleans
2. Kathy Wilkerson
3. Molly, New York City
4. Hudson River
5. Boston Post Road
6. Tony, September
7. town, miles
8. month
9. voice, style
10. woman, books
11. boy, radio
12. saxophone, horn
13. home
14.–18. Answers will vary.

MASTER 3: VERBS 1
1. adopted
2. call
3. grabs, thrusts
4. astonishes
5. broke
6. suffered
7. retired
8. fascinate
9. keep
10. live
11. weighs
12. raised
13. ordered
14. stare
15.–24. Answers will vary. Sample answers:
15. lose
16. take
17. finish
18. frown
19. agree
20. shout
21. follow
22. freeze
23. empty
24. write

MASTER 4: VERBS 2
1. past
2. present
3. past
4. present
5. future
6. future
7. plays
8. earned
9. received
10. competes
11. will talk
12. will organize
13. moves; moved *or* will move
14. jumped; jumps *or* will jump
15. captured; captures *or* will capture
16. selects; selected *or* will select
17. will force; forces *or* forced

MASTER 5: ADJECTIVES 1
1. first
2. largest, southern
3. major, sweet
4. delicate, oval
5. juicy, late
6. great
7. fresh
8. muddy
9. wailing
10. exhausted
11. lucky
12.–16. Answers will vary.

MASTER 6: ADJECTIVES 2
1. Green, busiest
2. urban, peaceful
3. One, cool
4. skinny, busy
5. frisky, dark, old
6. Red, western, leafy
Answers will vary. Sample answers:
7. pretty, red
8. brave, young
9. old, yellow
10. shy, friendly
11.–15. Answers will vary.

MASTER 7: ADVERBS 1
1. regularly
2. well
3. often
4. bitterly
5. later
6. wisely
7. gratefully
8. swiftly
9. famously, there
10. bravely
11. nearly
12. now
13.–20. Answers will vary.

MASTER 8: ADVERBS 2
1. fearlessly
2. there
3. Remarkably
4. everywhere
5. once
6. Now
7. usually
8. slowly
9. Here
10. fearlessly
11. Remarkably
12. slowly
13. once
14. Now
15. usually
16. there
17. everywhere
18. Here
19.–23. Answers will vary. Sample answers:
19. often
20. graciously
21. thoroughly
22. proudly
23. loudly